Encountering the Lord
in Daily Life

Msgr. David E. Rosage

LIVING FLAME PRESS
LOCUST VALLEY, N.Y. 11560

All Scripture quotations are taken from the New American Bible

Nihil Obstat: Rev. Armand M. Nigro, S.J.

Imprimatur: Most Rev. Lawrence H. Welsh, D.D.
                Bishop of Spokane

ISBN: 0-914544-45-4

COVER: Robert Manning

Copyright 1983: David E. Rosage

Published by Living Flame Press/Locust Valley/New York 11560

Printed in the United States of America.

CONTENTS

INTRODUCTION

From our earliest years many of us thought of God as "up there" and "out there." We usually visualized him as the transcendent God of the whole universe and only remotely present in the world in which we live.

Indeed he is a transcendent God of might and majesty, but he is also an immanent God—a loving Father who says to us: "I will welcome you and be a father to you and you will be my sons and daughters." How vividly he speaks of his presence: "I will dwell with them and walk among them. I will be their God and they shall be my people" *(II Cor. 6:16)*.

Jesus gives us a little glimpse into his mysterious presence when he states an essential condition for his indwelling:

> "Anyone who loves me will be true to my word, and my Father will love him; we will come to him and make our dwelling place with him" *(Jn. 14:23)*.

Jesus is living with us and within us in his glorified, risen life. We are his temples—members of his Body. While his presence is mysterious, it is, nonetheless, real.

Contemplating this consoling mystery, St. Paul exclaimed: "...the life I live now is not my own; Christ is living in me" (Gal. 2:20). Our goal in life, then, is to establish a rich, dynamic, personal relationship with the risen Jesus abiding with us at every moment of the day.

This series of unrelated happenings is a journal of events which call to mind the presence of the Lord in our daily living. The Lord is always with us and within us, but we often find it difficult to keep ourselves aware of his abiding presence as we become engrossed in the mundane and temporal preoccupations of every day.

Someone asked: "If God seems far away, who do you think moved?" The answer is obvious, for Jesus promised: "I will not leave you orphaned..." (Jn. 14:18). How comforting are his words: "know that I am with you always, until the end of the world!" (Mt. 28:20).

Our gracious Father's love is on-going. He is dynamically present in all of his creation—saturating, energizing, sustaining everything he made. Therefore, "In him we live and move and have our being" (Acts 17:28).

It is our prayerful intention that with God's inspiration and guidance, the isolated events recorded in the following pages may keep us more and more aware of his abiding and loving presence. May this journal of events aid us in walking more consciously with him wherever our daily duties may lead us.

To this end, we offer these 52 encounters with the Lord—one for each week of the year. The suggested scriptural texts which follow each presentation are intended to serve as a starting point, a guideline for our daily prayer. It would be fruitful to read and reflect on them as they appear in context in the Bible. For this reason we offer the reference for each one.

May these simple reflections help us find God in all things and may they redound to his greater honor and glory.

Feast of the Visitation May 31, 1983

1

MORNING STAR

I live in the land of sunrise and sunset. My home is on the western side of a mountain. Early in the morning the rising sun sends its bright rosy rays over the crest of the mountain alerting my part of the world that a new day is being born. As the sun continues to rise, it gradually brightens the little world around me.

As the sun climbs higher into the azure blue sky, it energizes my spirits, envelops me with its warmth and pours forth its brilliance into my heart.

Lingering to gaze at the rising sun, I can more easily enter into a contemplative prayer mood, as I begin to experience the presence of the Lord in the glorious dawn of a new day. Did not Jesus himself say: "I am . . . the Morning Star shining bright" (Rev. 22:16)?

St. Peter, using this same image of the rising sun, encourages us to linger with the prophetic message.

He urges us: "Keep your attention closely fixed on it, as you would on a lamp shining in a dark place until the first streaks of dawn appear and the morning star rises in your hearts" (II Pet. 1:19).

Furthermore, Jesus illumined the pathway for us in the predawn of a new day by his own example. After a busy day of teaching and healing, he began the new day—"Rising early the next morning, he went off to a lonely place in the desert; there he was absorbed in prayer" (Mk. 1:35).

As the sun continues to rise, clocking off the morning hours, I must leave my hallowed spot to plunge into the demanding activities of the day. I pray that the Morning Star may continue to rise in my heart.

This recurring birth of light each morning reminds me of all that Jesus expects of his followers. "You are the light of the world. A city set on a hill cannot be hidden. Men do not light a lamp and then put it under a bushel basket. They set it on a stand where it gives light to all in the house. In the same way, your light must shine before men so that they see goodness in your acts and give praise to your heavenly Father" (Mt. 5:14–16).

Each morning I must come to the Lord for a recharging of my battery so that my light may not only glow, but that I may be like "the Morning Star shining bright" in that area I call my world.

There Jesus will remind us that a gracious smile, a kind word, a thoughtful deed, a sincere thank you are only a few of the sparks that will burst into bright light radiating his love, peace and joy to everyone whose lives we touch that day.

As I gather myself together for another day, I am reminded of the Chinese proverb popularized by the

Christophers: "It is better to light one candle than to curse the darkness."

I am encouraged because even my candle glow in God's divine providence will bear some fruit. Our candle glow will blaze on into a flame as we ponder the love and life of the Lord radiating through his Word.

Psalm 50:1-"God the Lord has spoken and summoned the earth, from the rising of the sun to its setting."

Matthew 10:27, 28-"What you hear in private, proclaim from the housetops. Do not fear those who deprive the body of life but cannot destroy the soul"

Sirach 26:16-"Like the sun rising in the Lord's heavens, the beauty of a virtuous wife is the radiance of her home."

Zechariah 8:7-"Thus says the Lord of hosts: Lo, I will rescue my people from the land of the rising sun, and from the land of the setting sun."

Malachi 1:11-"For from the rising of the sun, even to its setting, my name is great among the nations. . ."

Luke 12:54-"He said to the crowds: 'When you see a cloud rising in the west, you say immediately that rain is coming-and so it does.' "

Judges 5:31-"May all your enemies perish thus, O

11

Lord! but your friends be as the sun rising in its might!''

2

MEDLEY OF PRAISE

The first moments of our morning awakening can be the most dichotomizing time of the whole day. For some people it is a dreadful moment of arousing oneself from a deep sleep; for others it is an exhilarating experience of greeting a brand new day. Those first moments are revealing, as they tell us something about our physical, psychological and even our spiritual personality.

Someone has said that there are two classes of morning-people: those who greet the new day with a cheerful and reverent "Good morning, God!"; and those who manage a weak and mumbled "Good God, morning?" One of my friends insists that she arises promptly at six o'clock but does not wake until about eight or nine o'clock.

Personally, I am doubly blessed. As soon as the first streaks of dawn appear, I awaken, fully conscious and alert. My second blessing is a special gift to me from God. Not far from my bedroom there are several large evergreen trees which keep their nightly vigil over me. I often awaken to the whispering of the gentle breeze in the pine branches, collaborating to sing their morning prayer to God.

Frequently I am greeted with a chorus of birds singing and warbling their hymn of praise to their Creator. The author of the book of Genesis reminds us that all creatures, even birds, are God's handiwork. "Then God said, '. . . on the earth let birds fly beneath the dome of the sky.' And so it happened: God created . . . all kinds of winged birds. God . . . blessed them, saying, . . . 'Let the birds multiply on the earth' "(Gen. 1:20–22).

God is present in all of his creation. He created the birds of the air, gifting them with the ability to sing, making them brilliant in appearance with their multicolored feathers, giving them sensation and the instinct to increase and multiply. The birds themselves seem to sense the goodness of their Creator and continue to serenade him with a chorus of praise all day long, but especially in the early morning hours.

The quail, who have been roosting in the needled branches of the evergreen trees, start their peculiar chatter. Since I do not understand bird language, I do not know if they are praising God, or if it is a predawn gossip session. At this morning hour birds of every kind and description add to this medley of praise with their lilting, chirping, singing.

In the distance I hear a proud rooster, not to be outdone, announcing to the world that morning has come. I can also hear the familiar voice of the meadow lark, chanting the same refrain over and over again, which seems to say, "David, Jesus loves you; David, Jesus loves you."

God loves all his creatures, for as the sacred writer tells us: "God looked at everything he had made and

13

found it very good" *(Gen. 1:31)*. Yet, I have an intuition that the Father loves birds in a special way. At the baptism of Jesus, " . . . the Holy Spirit descended on him in visible form like a dove" *(Lk. 3:22)*.

Did not Jesus single out birds when he was speaking of his provident Father's caring love? "Look at the birds in the sky. They do not sow or reap, they gather nothing into barns; yet your heavenly Father feeds them." In spite of his great love for birds, the Father loves us even more, for Jesus concluded with "Are you not more important than they?" *(Mt. 6:26)*.

The inspired writers often lead us into a medley of praise to the Lord. As we lift our minds and hearts to him, praise will echo from our lips.

Sirach 43:29-"Let us praise him the more, since we cannot fathom him, for greater is he than all his works"

Psalm 9:2,3-"I will give thanks to you, O Lord, with all my heart; I will declare all your wondrous deeds. I will be glad and exult in you; I will sing praise to your name, Most High"

Isaiah 12:5-"Sing praise to the Lord for his glorious achievement; let this be known throughout all the earth."

Matthew 11:25-"Father, Lord of heaven and earth, to you I offer praise; for what you have hidden from the learned and the clever you have revealed to the merest children."

Ephesians 1:3-"Praised be the God and Father of our

*Lord Jesus Christ, who has bestowed on us in
Christ every spiritual blessing in the heavens!''*

*Hebrews 13:15-"Through him let us continually of-
fer God a sacrifice of praise, that is, the fruit of lips
which acknowledge his name.''*

*Revelation 7:12-". . . . Praise the glory, wisdom and
thanksgiving and honor, power and might, to our
God forever and ever. Amen.''*

3

ROYALTY

One day a friend of mine called to make an ap-
pointment to discuss a problem. Her difficulty, like
millions of other people, was a poor self-image; she
had a severe inferiority complex. Many of the ven-
tures she had attempted in life had failed, which
crushed her ego and fragmented her self-confidence.
Added to these failures was her conviction that many
of her friends had rejected her. Her self-image was
not only down on the floor level, but it was all the
way under the carpet.

When my friend arrived at the appointed hour, I
greeted her with a cheery "Hi Princess!" She inter-
preted my greeting as being tinted with ridicule. She

thought I was trying to be facetious. As you would expect, this made her very indignant and angry.

I apologized and went on to explain that I really did not mean my greeting to be taken in a pejorative sense because she is in reality a princess. I reminded her that her heavenly Father is a King, the Lord of heaven and earth. In Baptism she became his adopted daughter, and therefore, she actually is a princess. I shared with her what St. Paul relayed to us: '' . . . You are the temple of the living God, just as God has said . . . 'I will welcome you and be a father to you and you will be my sons and daughters' . . . '' *(II Cor. 6:16–18).*

My friend looked at me rather skeptically, but her anger was subsiding. I continued the same line of thought. In another place, St. Paul reminds us again of this great privilege: "All who are led by the Spirit of God are the sons (and daughters) of God" *(Rom. 8:14).*

I risked addressing her as princess again as I went on to explain, "Princess, you love the Lord dearly and you have dedicated your whole life to him. Well, then, you are the person of whom St. John speaks: "Any who did accept him he empowered to become children of God" *(Jn. 1:12).*

I pursued the course of reasoning a little further when I explained that in my humble opinion, most people walking the face of the earth have a poor self-image. Most of us are unhappy with ourselves. We wish we had additional gifts and talents. We often try to conceal our age, and employ a host of other disguises to shield ourselves from what we think might be a rejection from others.

We also react in other ways. We may try to put our

best foot forward, wearing many different kinds of masks. Some resort to becoming a name-dropper. At times we may build a wall around ourselves so that others may not come too close, for fear that they may discover the real person we are and then reject us. All this facading creates tension and anxiety within us and contributes to our unhappiness.

What is the solution? How can we change our attitude? I think there is one sure panacea, and that begins with God. If we come to know God as our loving Father who created and gifted us, above all that he loves us just as we are, then we will be able to accept ourselves as we are.

Does God actually tell us that he loves us? Listen to his words: "... you are precious in my eyes and glorious and I ... love you" (Is. 43:4). And again: "With age-old love I have loved you" (Jer. 31:3).

Does he really care what happens to us? Listen to him as he speaks to your heart: "... I know well the plans I have in mind for you, says the Lord, plans for your welfare, not for woe! Plans to give you a future full of hope" (Jer. 29:11). These reassurances are legion throughout God's Word. Prayerfully listening to God expressing his love for us is the most effective attitudinal adjustment possible.

It has been several years now since my friend and I met to discuss her problem, but suffice it to say that every time she writes to me, she signs her name "Princess".

1 Peter 2:9-"You, however, are a 'chosen race, a royal priesthood, a holy nation, a people he claims...' "

Isaiah 49:15-16-"I will never forget you. See, upon the palms of my hands I have written your name;"

Psalm 5:3-"Heed my call for help, my king and my God!"

Psalm 97:1-"The Lord is king; let the earth rejoice;"

1 Timothy 1:17-"To the King of ages, the immortal, the invisible, the only God, be honor and glory forever and ever!"

Galatians 4:6-"The proof that you are sons is the fact that God has sent forth into our hearts the spirit of his Son which cries out 'Abba!' ('Father!')."

Revelation 17:14-"They will fight against the Lamb but the Lamb will conquer them, for he is the Lord of Lords and the King of Kings; victorious, too, will be his followers-the ones who were called: the chosen and the faithful."

4

UP AND DOWN APOSTOLATE

Recently I was visiting some patients in a large hospital. When I visit patients, I am in the habit of starting on the top floor and working my way down, floor by floor. This day my first stop was on the seventh floor.

I pushed the button to summon the elevator. It arrived in record time. When the doors opened to welcome me aboard, I saw that it was nearly filled. It was so crowded that I could not reach the panel to push number seven, so I asked the person beside me to punch seven for me. I thanked her graciously, but was greeted with a dead silence. Nor was there any conversation among the rest of the passengers as we stopped and started, floor after floor until we reached the seventh floor.

This experience was not unusual. It has happened to me consistently over the years. Each time I step into an elevator, I seem to be greeted with an awkward, embarrassed silence. I try to be pleasant and cheerful and make some small talk, but most of the time the only response I get is an uncomfortable silence. In such a confined space, silence weighs heavily. However, when I do get a response, the whole imprisoned audience seems to relax.

I ask myself why? There are many reasons, I am sure. Perhaps the passengers are occupied with their own thoughts and problems. Some may be shy or bashful, arising from the fear of exposing themselves or the lack of trust in other people. Others do not want to get involved. Some are reserved and reticent. The reasons, I am sure, are many.

Be that as it may, I feel that it is quite un-Christian; hence, I began to make it my personal apostolate to try to relieve the awkward chill of the typical elevator greeting. St. Peter gives us some paternal advice when he encourages us: ''Greet one another with the embrace of true love" *(1 Pet. 5:14).*

How many times St. Paul urges us to be cheerful and to greet one another as brothers and sisters in the Lord. Listen to some of his admonitions: "Do everything with love" *(1 Cor. 16:14).* He also expatiates on the qualities of Christian love: "Love is kind. . . . it does not put on airs, it is not snobbish. Love is never rude," *(1 Cor. 13:4, 5);* and today he would add "especially in the close confines of an elevator." I am sure that people are not intentionally rude or snobbish, even though it would appear so on the surface. One of the many areas where we are called to witness to Jesus, to radiate his joy and loving concern, is in elevators. I think this is especially true of elevators in hospitals, because there we find many people with heavy hearts.

For those who wish to join the elevator apostolate, the following Scriptures may be helpful.

Ephesians 5:21-"Defer to one another out of reverence for Christ."

Colossians 4:6-"Let your speech be always gracious and in good taste, and strive to respond properly to all who address you."

1 Thessalonians 5:14-". . . cheer the fainthearted; support the weak; be patient toward all."

Galatians 6:2-"Help carry one another's burdens; in that way you will fulfill the law of Christ."

Romans 12:8-"He who gives alms should do so generously; he who rules should exercise his

authority with care; he who performs works of
mercy should do so cheerfully."

Sirach 30:22-"Gladness of heart is the very life of
man, cheerfulness prolongs his days."

Matthew 5:47-". . . if you greet your brothers only,
what is so praiseworthy about that? Do not pagans
do as much?"

5

FEAR IS USELESS

How often someone will admit that they find it
very difficult to trust God implicitly. How often we
find ourselves in the same predicament! Most of us,
I am sure, have been confronted with this dilemma
many times in our lives. We want to trust God, and
we try hard to have full confidence in him and his
plans for us, but we hesitate. We have so many
misgivings. We may wonder at times if God is really concerned about the problems and the pains in
our lives. Our hearts reassure us that we should trust
him, but our pragmatic minds keep conjuring up all
sorts of doubts, fears, worries and anxieties.

On the other hand we may have found ourselves

in a situation which was beyond our control. In our helplessness we may have been compelled to throw ourselves into God's arms, calling upon his providential love to rescue us. In such instances we may have been astonished how graciously our loving Father responded to our plea by resolving our problem and how effectively he removed all those imaginary barriers from our path.

Thus we discover once again that our caring, concerned Father proves his fidelity to his promise: "For I know well the plans I have in mind for you, says the Lord, plans for your welfare, not for woe! plans to give you a future full of hope. When you call me, when you go to pray to me, I will listen to you. When you look for me, you will find me. Yes, when you seek me with all your heart, you will find me with you, says the Lord, and I will change your lot" (Jer. 29:11–14).

During his earthly sojourn Jesus constantly urged us to place complete trust in his Father and in him. In picturesque language he pleaded with us to trust him. On one occasion when he was encouraging us to dispel all fear he used this illustration:

"Are not two sparrows sold for next to nothing? Yet not a single sparrow falls to the ground without your Father's consent. As for you, every hair of your head has been counted; so do not be afraid of anything. You are worth more than an entire flock of sparrows" Mt. 10:29-31).

A friend of mine told me that expressions such as 'Fear not' or 'Do not be afraid' are used some three hundred sixty-six times in Scripture. He concluded that this is one for each day of the year and one extra one for leap year. If this is so, then I believe God is trying to tell us each day that we should never be afraid; that we should trust him.

In Sacred Scripture we also find that when God is active and dynamic in someone's life, we always find a little admonition not to be afraid. When the angel appeared to our Blessed Mother, he allayed her fears with: "Do not fear, Mary. You have found favor with God" *(Lk. 1:30)*.

On another occasion when the apostles were floundering in the midst of a storm on the Sea of Galilee, Jesus approached them with the words; "It is I; do not be afraid" *(Jn. 6:20)*.

After his resurrection Jesus repeatedly dispelled all fears of his strange and sudden appearances with the words: "Peace be with you."

Frequently Jesus assured us that the Father loves us and that he himself loves us with an infinite love. His words are convincing: "The Father already loves you, because you have loved me and have believed that I came from God" *(Jn. 16:27)*. Then Jesus tells us of his own love for us: "As the Father has loved me, so I have loved you" *(Jn. 15:9)* . The collorary is quite evident. If God loves us and if we love him, there is "no room for fear; rather, perfect love casts out all fear" *(I Jn. 4:18)*.

As we let Jesus' words find a home in our heart, it will cast out all fear.

Luke 12:32-"Do not live in fear, little flock."

Luke 8:50-"Fear is useless; what is needed is trust . . ."

John 14:1–3-"Have faith in God and faith in me...."

Luke 2:10-"You have nothing to fear! I come to proclaim good news to you-tidings of great joy to be shared by the whole people."

Mark 10:49-"You have nothing to fear from him!"

1 Peter 3:13–14-"Fear not and do not stand in awe of what this people fears..."

Romans 8:15-"You did not receive a spirit of slavery leading you back into fear, but a spirit of adoption through which we cry out, 'Abba' (that is, 'Father')."

6

LISTENING TO THE QUAIL

In the building where I live there is an extended overhang which serves as a patio-type protection from the rain and snow. During the winter months this sheltered area has become a haven for the quail to come and eat. Under this protection, the quail come in huge numbers, searching for food.

What a joy to feed them each day and to watch

them munching the grain placed there for them. As I listen I have never been able to decipher their chattering as they peck away at the scattered grain. Nor have I ever been able to count them since they dart back and forth so quickly.

In the early fall these quail are easily frightened, nervous and jittery. They will fly away at the least movement or noise. Gradually, they become more domesticated and are less easily threatened. I like to think that they are beginning to trust us more and more, and that they realize that we are not going to harm them, but rather wish to provide food for their survival.

These quail remind me of our attitude toward the transcendent God of heaven and earth. Most of us look upon God with awe and reverence. Like the quail, we live with a certain fear of him. How frequently we lack trust in him because he may expect too much from us.

In his providential love, the Father has supplied all our needs. So many of these we simply take for granted without realizing that they are special gifts from our caring Father. As we reflect on our loving Father's benevolence to us, we recognize that we lack for nothing.

Gradually we begin to trust him more and more. As we prayerfully listen to his Word, we hear him telling us that he has plans for our welfare, not for woe (Jer. 29:11ff). We hear Jesus assuring us: "Your heavenly Father knows all that you need. Seek first his kingship over you, his way of holiness, and all these things will be given you besides" (Mt. 6:32, 33). Again, we are reminded that every hair on our head is counted—that's how precious we are to him

(Mt. 10:30).

In the fall of the year, as we start feeding the quail, only a few are brave enough to come to eat. They are easily frightened. However, as "the word" gets around, the bevy increases drastically in numbers and so does their courage. They seem to have invited the whole 'relationship' to come to enjoy the feast prepared for their survival.

We can draw another parallel from this fact. When we begin to count our manifold blessings, our trust in the heavenly Father's providential concern for us increases. As we enjoy the goodness of God, we want to spread the good news of his kindness. We need to tell others and draw them into a deeper appreciation of his care and concern for them.

This is our apostolate in life. Just as the quail not only come themselves, but encourage the whole bevy to come to eat, so must we reach out in loving concern to others, especially to those who do not have sufficient confidence and trust in our heavenly Father's faithfulness and love.

Our provident Father invites us to meet him in his Word—there to find reassurance that he cares for us.

Jeremiah 29:11–14-"For I know well the plans I have in mind for you. . . ."

Matthew 6:26-". . . are not you more important than they?"

Psalm 23-"The Lord is my shepherd; I shall not want. . . ."

John 3:16–18-"Yes, God so loved the world that he gave his only Son, . . ."

John 14:23-"we will come to him and make our dwelling place with him. . . . "

Romans 8:28–39-"If God is for us, who can be against us?. . . . "

John 1:1–18-"Any who did accept him he empowered to become children of God. . . . "

7

BUTTERCUPS

One balmy spring morning I was taking a walk in the country to enjoy the beauty of the day which the Lord had made.

As I strolled on the soft, warm blanket of God's good earth, I saw that it was dotted with gold-like nuggets glistening in the morning sunshine. Buttercups had emerged with their waxen faces smiling up at me. Hundreds of them were generously sprinkled over the whole terrain.

Never before had buttercups spoken so eloquently to me. My first impression was: "What a pity—these precious flowers are so small and so far removed that they cannot be admired far and wide by all of God's people. What a pity that they are in this isolated spot, 'wasting their sweetness on the desert air'!"

No, it was not a waste. They were not living in vain. This morning they were raising their tiny faces heavenward to praise their Creator by simply being buttercups. Are we not all created to love, reverence, praise and serve our Creator and Father?

Secondly, this morning they were being buttercups just for me. I needed to see them, to recognize them as one of the myriad creations of God, just for me. I needed to be reminded that God loves me so much he has made everything for my use and enjoyment. Yes, even buttercups can lead me onward and upward to my loving Father.

These buttercups reminded me, too, that Jesus loves the "anawim"—the little people. "Father, Lord of heaven and earth, to you I offer praise; for what you have hidden from the learned and the clever you have revealed to the merest children" *(Mt. 11:25).*

Jesus, how lowly was your Mother in the eyes of the world! How humble your own birth according to secular standards! How unimportant were your apostles! How insignificant in worldly eyes were all your disciples. Down through the ages, how very precious in your sight was the whole host of "little people."

It is a reminder, again, that "what" we do in this life is not as important as we sometimes think. All-important is the "why." And the "why" is love.

As I wended my way back homeward, I stepped carefully so that I would not crush those precious little buttercups. Once more I looked back at God's blanket of earth, so artistically spotted with gold in little flowers. "Thank you, Father, for buttercups."

Matthew 6:28-"Learn a lesson from the way the wild flowers grow . . ."

28

Sirach 16:22–28-"the Lord looked upon the earth, and filled it with his blessings."

Sirach 40:22-"Charm and beauty delight the eye, but better than either, the flowers of the field."

1 Peter 1:24-". . . . The grass withers, the flower wilts, but the word of the Lord endures forever."

Mark 6:40-"The people took their places in hundreds and fifties, neatly arranged like flower beds. . . ."

Job 14:2-"Like a flower that springs up and fades, swift as a shadow that does not abide. . . ."

Psalm 147:1-"Praise the Lord, for he is good; sing praise to our God, for he is gracious; it is fitting to praise him."

8

DAWN OF A SPRING MORNING

Have the first rays of sunshine on a spring morning ever tantalized you to get up to begin a new day? Have they awakened in you new hope and great expectancy as nature awakes from its wintry sleep? In early morning the gloom of night is gradually dissipated by the first glimmer of the sun glowing in the East. At first we might see only dim outlines of objects, and then slowly they come into sharper focus as the darkness is dispelled.

Life in this land of exile follows similar patterns. In the springtime of life we experience some uncertainty and insecurity. At times we cannot see the path which the Lord is mapping out for us. Our way is often quite dark, or at best dimly lit.

St. Paul describes our plight in these words: "Now we see indistinctly, as in a mirror; then we shall see face to face. My knowledge is imperfect now; then I shall know even as I am known" (1 Cor. 13:12).

Just as the early morning sun rises to light our way, so Jesus came into our world to show us the way to our eternal home. He said of himself:

"I am the way, and the truth, and the life; no one comes to the Father but through me" (Jn. 14:6).

Jesus comes into our life as the light of the world. He identifies himself in these words: "It is I, . . . Jesus, the Morning Star shining bright" (Rev. 22:16).

Jesus is not only the Morning Star, but the warm, brilliant noonday sun in our lives. We cannot see clearly in a darkened room. However, our vision is much improved as we step out into the sunshine. When we are close to Jesus it is always high noon.

On our spiritual journey, the closer we come to Jesus the better will we recognize the plan and purpose of God in our lives. As we bask in the sunshine of his presence, we enjoy the warmth of his love, the uplifting of our spirit and the nourishment of body and soul, so essential to our journey. Likewise, in the light of his presence, we more easily discern those influences which would lead us off on devious tangents.

In the springtime of life our pathway may be dimly lit, but as the "Morning Star, shining bright" appears, we can see more clearly that our path is not only on solid ground but that it is also leading us directly to the Father.

The following Scriptures will not only lead us along the right path, but will continue to support us as we journey alone.

John 8:12-"No follower of mine shall ever walk in darkness; . . . "

Matthew 5:14–16-"You are the light of the world. . . . "

Isaiah 49:6-". . . . I will make you a light to the nations, that my salvation may reach to the ends of the earth."

John 1:4, 5-"Whatever came to be in him, found life, life for the light of men. The light shines on in darkness, a darkness that did not overcome it."

John 3:19-". . . the light came into the world, but men loved darkness rather than light because their deeds were wicked."

Ephesians 6:18-"At every opportunity pray in the

Spirit, using prayers and petitions of every sort.
Pray constantly and attentively. . . . "

Mark 1:35-"Rising early the next morning, he (Jesus)
went off to a lonely place in the desert; there he
was absorbed in prayer."

9

MY FATHER'S HOUSE

Birthdays are annual events which we observe
with mixed emotions. We celebrate them with
gladness and gratitude and yet there lingers within
us a kind of foreboding. Birthdays are a reminder that
we are getting older. We fear old age not only
because of the limitations and infirmities it brings
with it, but mostly because it reminds us of the certainty of the end of our earthly existence.

We don't like to think about our own death. In
fact, we somehow harbor the notion that death may
not happen in our case. We may be the one excep-
tion to this universal law.

We take every precaution to ward off the threat of
death. We become antiseptically, hygienically and
medically solicitous about our physical well-being.

There is in every human heart an insatiable desire
to know more about life after death, to learn more

about what happens to us beyond the grave. This desire arises not only from a natural curiosity, but also from a fear of the unknown.

Intellectually we know that God loves us and wants to share his love, his goodness and his happiness with us for all eternity. But this knowledge is often overshadowed by a sense of our own sinfulness, our own unworthiness to receive his love. Fortunately God does not wait until we are worthy of his love. He loves us just as we are in spite of all our waywardness. St. John is speaking to each one of us personally when he says: "Love, then, consists in this: not that we have loved God, but that he has loved us..." *(1 Jn. 4:10).* If the beloved disciple does not allay all our fears, listen to how compassionately Jesus prepares us for the fullness of our resurrected life, and encourages us to trust him:

"Do not let your hearts be troubled. Have faith in God and faith in me....I am indeed going to prepare a place for you, and then I shall come back to take you with me, that where I am you also may be" *(Jn. 14:1–3).*

We begin to live our resurrected life at the moment of our Baptism. It is augmented within us as we live our sacramental life more fully. Death is our entrance into glory when the Trinity shares more fully its divine life with us.

How often we are reassured of this truth in God's Word.

Romans 6:3-5-"If we have been united with him through likeness to his death, so shall we be through a like resurrection."

John 17:24-"Father, all those you gave me I would have in my company where I am, to see this glory of mine. . . ."

1 Corinthians 2:9-"Eye has not seen, ear has not heard, nor has it so much as dawned on man what God has prepared for those who love him."

John 6:54-"He who feeds on my flesh and drinks my blood has life eternal, and I will raise him up on the last day."

John 6:37-"All that the Father gives me shall come to me; no one who comes will I ever reject."

Romans 8:11-"If the Spirit of him who raised Jesus from the dead dwells in you, then he who raised Christ from the dead will bring your mortal bodies to life also through his Spirit dwelling in you."

1 Corinthians 15:54, 55-"Death is swallowed up in victory. O death, where is your victory? O death, where is your sting?"

10

NOT EVEN A BARN

Joe is a devout Catholic. He is now retired and assists at Mass daily. He is finding changes in the Liturgy rather painful, and at times even rather devastating. He does not like the music; he misses the quiet time to be alone with the Lord. For Joe, there seems to be all too much irreverence in our churches. To say the least, he is very much disillusioned in these days of his retirement when he longs to be a daily communicant.

I often wonder how I can bring Joe some comfort and reassurance; how I can help him to become more open and receptive and to find more peace in the evening of his life.

As I was trying to empathize with Joe and find some approach to his problem, I went back in spirit to Galilee to the time of Jesus. On a barren hillside, the flowers and grass are all dried up. A dusty road, clogged with people, traverses the slope of the hill. The so-called roadway is filled with stones, holes and droppings from the beasts of burden, as well as from sheep and goats. The crowd is noisy. Some merchants are shouting as they try to sell their wares. A few travelling minstrels are hoping for some generous gratuities as they sing their popular ballads. Children are screaming their delight as they play their games, while others are waiting out of fear for more attention.

On the rocky terrain, there is a gathering of people. The teacher's chair which Jesus uses is a hard, rough rock. People are sitting on the barren dusty ground or on the shaded side of a huge rock. Others are squatting or standing around. All eyes are riveted on Jesus. There is no shelter against the burning sun or the scorching wind blowing off the desert. The noise rises and falls. Amid the crescendos and decrescendos, Jesus' voice comes through loud and clear: "Love your enemies, pray for your persecutors." *(Mt. 5:44).*

As I ponder this scene I am lifted in spirit to the Upper Room where Jesus is about to give himself Eucharistically to us and to the world. He begins the penitential rite with the washing of the feet of his disciples. I notice that his only vestment is a towel around his waist.

Along the Via Dolorosa, Jesus is pushed, shoved and dragged along the narrow, filth-littered streets leading to Calvary. The noise is raucous. The shouts blasphemous.

Next I find myself at Jacob's Well, listening as Jesus explains to the Samaritan woman: "Believe me, woman, an hour is coming when you will worship the Father neither on this mountain (Gerizim) nor in Jerusalem. . . . authentic worshipers will worship the Father in Spirit and truth"*(Jn. 4:21–23).*

I remind myself, as I have often told Joe, that we must focus on essentials. We must penetrate beyond the surface. We must see beyond the periphery. We must recognize the voice of Jesus amid the din of everyday traffic. We must not close the door in Jesus' face when he comes to us in poor, unconventional attire.

Jesus did not even have a barn in which to gather his disciples. He himself reminds us that "the Son of Man has nowhere to lay his head" *(Mt. 8:20)*.

Mark 1:35-"Rising early the next morning, he went off to a lonely place in the desert; there he was absorbed in prayer."

Luke 9:28-"he (Jesus) took Peter, John and James, and went up onto a mountain to pray."

Isaiah 56:7-"Them I will bring to my holy mountain and make joyful in my house of prayer. . . ."

Luke 2:7-"She gave birth to her first-born son and wrapped him in swaddling clothes and laid him in a manger, because there was no room for them in the place where travelers lodged."

Matthew 21:12–16-"My house shall be called a house of prayer, but you are turning it into a den of thieves. . . ."

Acts 16:11–15-"Once, on the sabbath, we went outside the city gate to the bank of the river, where we thought there would be a place of prayer. . . ."

Matthew 5:23–24-". . . Leave your gift at the altar, go first to be reconciled with your brother. . ."

11

A GOOD SAMARITAN WITHOUT A DONKEY

Most of us anxiously await the daily newscasts in order to satisfy our insatiable curiosity about what is happening in the world, and also to keep ourselves informed of the events and developments in our society.

I am sure that most of us come away from these telecasts or radio reports a little saddened and disappointed, maybe even disheartened and discouraged. There seems to be such a profusion of bad news which counteracts any mention of good news.

In the midst of this situation we must be careful that we do not lose our sense of humor or our faith in human nature.

We must keep reminding ourselves that people are basically good. They want to love their fellow man, but sometimes they are afraid. Furthermore, we know that God, in his providential love, can and does bring much good out of chaos.

Not long ago I had a unique experience of the goodness of people. I was driving along a country road up in the mountains. Suddenly the oil filter blew a gasket, and all the oil ran out of the engine. It was impossible to drive any farther.

I did not even have time to consider what my next move would be, before a pickup truck came by and the driver stopped to offer assistance. This young man towed me many miles to a garage. There we found that the mechanic had gone home. My Good Samaritan who had towed me all this way told me that the mechanic was known to him and that he would call him at his home.

The mechanic agreed to come back to the garage to help me in my plight. In a short time the damage was repaired, and I was ready to be on my way.

When I offered to pay the person who had towed me those many miles, he simply told me to return the favor when I found some person stranded along the road.

The mechanic charged me only for the oil he used to refill my engine. He likewise said that he would not take advantage of a person who was in a predicament and would accept nothing for his labor.

There are still many Good Samaritans around, and they do much to restore faith in human nature by reflecting their loving concern for their neighbors.

Thank God for all Good Samaritans!

Would you like to be a Good Samaritan? These suggested reflections will create the Good Samaritan attitude in you which will eventually become a habit pattern. "Then go and do the same." (Lk. 10:25:37).

Luke 6:36–38-"Be compassionate, as your Father is compassionate."

Luke 9:48-". . . 'Whoever welcomes this little child on my account welcomes me,. . . the least one among you is the greatest.' "

Acts 2:42–45-"They devoted themselves to the

apostles' instruction and the communal life, to the breaking of bread and the prayers. . . . "

1 Timothy 6:18-"Charge them to do good, to be rich in good works and generous, sharing what they have."

Matthew 7:12-"Treat others the way you would have them treat you: this sums up the law and the prophets."

Tobit 4:16-"Give to the hungry some of your bread, and to the naked some of your clothing. . . . "

Matthew 25:40-". . . . I assure you, as often as you did it for one of my least brothers, you did it for me ."

12

THE MODEL SURFER

Time spent at the beach can be a deep, contemplative experience. The expansiveness of the ocean, the power concealed in its billowing waves reminds us of the omnipotent might of God who holds the entire ocean in the palm of his hand like a tiny drop of water. The prophet defines one phase of God's power in these few words:

"Who has cupped in his hand the water of the sea" (Is. 40:12).

As we walk along the beach, the surf lapping at our feet calls to mind the touch of God's love. If we frolic in the ocean, the restless water invigorates us. An occasional wave may inundate us, reminding us that the deluge of God's love floods our lives at all times. At every moment of our life, we are bathing in the ocean of his love.

There is much to be said about the joy of surfing. A proficient surfer continues to paddle his way out into the ocean riding the waves or plunging through them until he has gained some distance from the shore. From this vantage point, he strives to ride the waves safely toward the beach.

In all the hills and valleys of life, we are like the surfer trying desperately to ride out the swells and waves—sometimes successfully, many times not. However, a good surfer never gives up. Even though he falls frequently, he tries again and again.

The perseverance of the surfer makes me ask myself about my own determination to rise after my many falls in life. Do I get discouraged in the face of difficulties and fall? More important, like a good surfer, do I rise and try again and again?

Jesus is the model surfer. His life is such a compelling example for all of us. How patiently and how successfully Jesus rode out all the waves of criticism, animosity and hatred leveled at him.

By his walking on the water and by his rescuing

Peter when he began to sink into the lake, Jesus assures us that no storm can overcome us if we trust in him. With Peter we need to cry out: "Lord, save me!"

Perhaps Jesus may respond to us as he did to Peter: "How little faith you have! Why did you falter?" Even though Peter's faith was weak, Jesus came to the rescue. The Evangelist says: "Jesus at once stretched out his hand and caught him" (Mt.14:22-31).

Jesus does the same for us. He may leave us to flounder for a time in order to make us aware of our total dependence on him, but he will never let us sink and go under the waves.

In the Gospel we discover how pleased and how thrilled Jesus is when he finds genuine faith in him. On the other hand he registers disappointment at the lack of faith.

This same Jesus is living with us and within us in his resurrected life. How happy he is when we accept him and all that happens to us with a dynamic, operative faith. A strong faith will keep us ever aware of his abiding presence with us in all the happenings of every day. This kind of faith will generate great confidence and trust within us, knowing that whatever happens is either the Lord's will for us, or he permits it to happen for our spiritual growth. This kind of faith has no room for worry, anxiety or discouragement, because we know that Jesus is concerned about even the tiniest detail of our lives. Does he not tell us that every hair on our head is numbered?

Like the seasoned surfer Jesus wants us to ride out every wave of disappointment, difficulty or discouragement. As a good surfer Jesus wants us to rise after every fall and try again and again until we reach the eternal shore.

His Word is an inexhaustible source of hope and encouragement to us in the midst of life's struggle. Let us listen with all our being as he speaks to our hearts.

Wisdom 3:9-"Those who trust in him shall understand truth, and the faithful shall abide with him
in love: Because grace and mercy are with his holy
ones, and his care is with his elect."

Jude 1:21-"Persevere in God's love, and welcome
the mercy of our Lord Jesus Christ which leads to
life eternal."

Psalm 101:2-"I will persevere in the way of integri-
ty; when will you come to me?"

Ephesians 6:16-"In all circumstances hold faith up
before you as your shield; it will help you ex-
tinguish the fiery darts of the evil one."

Matthew 21:21,22-"Jesus said: 'Believe me, if you
trust and do not falter, not only will you do what
I did to the fig tree, but if you say to this mountain, 'Be lifted up and thrown into the sea' even
that will happen. You will receive all that you pray
for, provided you have faith.' "

Luke 8:15-"The seed on good ground are those who
hear the word in a spirit of openness, retain it, and
bear fruit through perseverance."

John 6:40—"Indeed this is the will of my Father, that everyone who looks upon the Son and believes in him shall have eternal life. Him I will raise up on the last day."

13

ONLY A WINDOW

A Melchite priest-friend of mine was showing me through his new parish church. I was overwhelmed by the profusion of icons which covered the walls and ceiling. I commented about the stereotypes which did not give the artist much freedom to use his creative talents and imagination.

My friend must have recognized my lack of artistic appreciation for this type of art. With a few well-chosen words he explained the purpose and method in these artistic creations. He put it this way: "If a person looks only at the surface, there seems to be great uniformity and perhaps a lack of originality. However, we are not merely to observe what readily meets the eye. The subject portrayed on the picture is only the window through which we look to the infinite. In our contemplative gaze we see through the picture to behold the divine. This is the prayer-posture we hope to achieve through our art."

As I pondered this informative explanation, I

thought of the myriad colorful posters and pictures which we find everywhere. Their subjects are beautifully and artistically presented, but their purpose goes much farther. The messages on these posters are pithy and pointed; often taken literally from the Word of God. Their purpose is much the same as the icons. We must look beyond the scene they portray to the God whose beauty is reflected in all his creation.

As we admire the exquisite beauty of a rural scene or a snow-capped mountain, or a lake or river, our spirit is lifted far above what our eyes behold. The picture is only the window through which we see the creative love of God radiating just one little aspect of his beauty through these inspiring images.

Who could gaze in awe at a rosy sunset, or the vastness of the restless ocean, or the grandeur of a mountain or the distinctive beauty of a desert without thinking of the transcendent God of heaven and earth? These attractive posters become our stepping-stones into a contemplative union with our loving Father. They serve as a launching pad into a deeper relationship with God. They are the elevator which raises us above the mundane.

This type of art speaks eloquently to us as it leads us into an other-worldly atmosphere. A picture may speak a thousand words; but, more important, these scenes lead us into a wordless communication with our God.

I rummaged through my personal "gem-book" to discover what Pius XII said about art.

"The function of all art lies in the fact while breaking through the narrow and tortuous enclosure of the finite in which man is immersed while living here below, it provides a window to the infinite for his hungry soul."

Jesus paints many verbal pictures for us in making known the Good News to our finite minds. Pause to behold the picture, but let your spirit penetrate beyond to the loving God who speaks to your heart.

The psalmist bids us look through the window of material creation to experience the love of our Creating Father.

Psalm 104:1, 2-"You are clothed with majesty and glory, robed in light as with a cloak."

V.10-"You send forth springs into the watercourses that wind among the mountains."

V.12-"Beside them the birds of heaven dwell; from among the branches they send forth their song."

V.16-"Well watered are the trees of the Lord. . ."

V.19-"You made the moon to mark the seasons; the sun knows the hour of its setting."

V.25-"The sea also, great and wide, in which are schools without number of living things both small and great, . . ."

V.27-"They all look to you to give them food in due time."

14

COMES THE DAWN

It was still very early when I was awakened by the rain rapping on my window, bidding me to get up and greet the new day. When I drew back the drapes I was staring into drippy darkness. The rainfilled clouds intensified the inky blackness.

As I began my prayer that morning I turned my chair to face the impenetrable darkness of the night—a darkness not yet willing to release its shroud over the earth to a new day. I could not make out even the dim outlines of anything out-of-doors, not even the graceful Douglas fir tree outside my window, which ordinarily waves a cheery 'good morning' to me. The darkness isolated me totally from my accustomed world.

I reflected how blind I am without Jesus, the Light of the world. Without his illumination I lose my whole perspective in life. Unless he shows me the way I flounder in my own self-centeredness. My own selfish whims and wishes often lead me astray when I shift my focus from Jesus.

As I gazed into the drizzling darkness, I prayed with blind Bartimaeus: "Rabboni, . . . I want to see." (Mk. 10:46–52). Yes, I am in the dark so often. I need the Lord's light and guidance. At times I am not at all certain what his will is for me.

As the minutes clicked off, I began to notice the

faint outlines of the familiar landscape outside my bedroom window. Gradually objects were taking shape. In due time, I could see the carpet of green lawn, the rainsoaked branches of the trees waving in the breeze as they shed their moisture drop by drop.

How correct was the writer when he penned: "I pray, then I understand." So often in my own life I can recall being faced with a problem or a decision for which there was no apparent solution. After I spent some time in prayer and placed the whole matter into the hands of the Lord, suddenly the answer came very clearly. First I had to learn to give it totally to the Lord in faith and trust.

Too often I try to find the solution, or strive to handle the whole matter myself. Only when I fail do I turn to the Lord. In the Gospel, it was only after the apostles admitted their own inability, or their inadequacy, that Jesus took over. Each day I need to step out with more confidence and trust in the Lord.

The psalmist's guidance is very timely: "Leave it to the Lord, and wait for him" *(Ps. 37:7).* Contemplating his Word will increase my trust and confidence.

John 14:1-"Do not let your hearts be troubled. . . . "

Mark 5:36-"Fear is useless; what is needed is trust."

Mark 10:46–52-"Rabboni, . . . I want to see."

Matthew 20:29–34-"Lord, . . . open our eyes!"

Psalm 37:5-"Commit to the Lord your way; trust in him, and he will act."

Mark 9:24-"I do believe! Help my lack of trust!"

John 8:12-"No follower of mine shall ever walk in darkness . . . ."

15

ONLY A SHADOW

A small group of us were sitting on a patio at my friend's home high on a mountainside. The view to the west was magnificent.

As the sun began to hasten toward the western horizon, it spread an exquisite glow over the whole sky. The setting sun painted the vast expanse of fleecy clouds with many and varied pinkish hues. Some of the tints faded while others grew more brilliant. The whole vault of heaven was a gigantic canopy of celestial beauty.

While we stood motionless and speechless, an awe and reverent quiet settled over our whole group. Silently we drank in this small phase of God's creation.

Finally one of the guests broke the silence with: "Imagine what God must be like! I wish I could hold this scene forever."

Another person, gifted with a sense of humor, cupped his hands before his mouth like a megaphone and pretended to shout: "Don't fret, Joe, I'll be back tomorrow with more of the same."

This light pretense of God responding was met with a hearty laugh, but it served its purpose. This remark reminded us that creation all too dimly reflects the beauty and sensitivity, the might and power of our loving Father. I wonder if the psalmist had just enjoyed a magnificent sunset when he sang:

"The heavens declare the glory of God and the firmament proclaims his handiwork" (Ps. 19:2).

It also reminded us that God is always with us, even though we are more aware of his presence on such occasions when he manifests the beauty of his creation so dramatically.

Didn't the Father assure us that he carries us in the palm of his hand, providing for us at each moment of the day? Each day we are reminded in myriad different ways of God's creative love.

A young mother tried to share with me the deep moving contemplative experience she enjoys each time she gives birth to another child. She spoke of the privilege of sharing in God's creative power in bringing another life into the world. It is awesome when we think that that person will live for all eternity.

A concert violinist thanks God every day for the gift and agility of his hands.

A postman is grateful for his ability to walk. He said that this sense of gratitude wells up in him each time he delivers mail to some person who is not ambulatory.

What have we in life that God has not created for

us, be it our sight, hearing or the many other faculties we enjoy? We can thank God by using well the gifts with which he has endowed us. The following Scriptures serve as reminders:

Psalm 8:2&10-"O Lord, our Lord, how glorious is your name over all the earth!"

Sirach 43:1,2-"The clear vault of the sky shines forth like heaven itself, a vision of glory. The orb of the sun, resplendent at its rising: what a wonderful work of the Most High!"

Psalm 113:3-"From the rising to the setting of the sun is the name of the Lord to be praised."

Psalm 119:175-"Let my soul live to praise you, and may your ordinances help me."

Psalm 104:1,2-". . . O Lord, my God, you are great indeed! You are clothed with majesty and glory, robed in light as with a cloak."

Matthew 11:25-"Father, Lord of heaven and earth, to you I offer praise; for what you have hidden from the learned and the clever you have revealed to the merest children."

Romans 7:19–25-". . . . All praise to God, through Jesus Christ our Lord! . . . "

16

CLOWNING FOR THE LORD

I know a clown personally. He is a very dignified and successful business man in my home town with a very unusual hobby. He takes time out regularly to perform as a clown whenever he is invited to do so. Few, if any, in the audience know his real identity. It would curtail his performance.

One day I had lunch with my clown-friend. After the business at hand was completed, I asked him about his hobby of clowning. He gave me some keen insights into this art.

He explained that everyone loves a clown, but not all know the real reason. A clown is loved not simply for his bizarre costume, not solely for his antics and gyrations, not for his jocular sense of humor alone. It goes much deeper than all of these externals.

One of the aims of a clown is to make people laugh and enjoy themselves. The performance of a clown may seem ludicrous and evoke outbursts of laughter and applause; however, his actions and movements are skillfully planned to look ridiculous.

The philosophy of a clown and his performance have a serious intent. People enjoy a clown because they recognize themselves in his mimicry. The clown tries to imitate people and portray them as they react to real life. He strives to show people how laughable are some of the things they do.

My friend went on to say that people, for the most part, take themselves too seriously. People get upset when their suggested mode of action is frowned upon. They often pout, withdraw and refuse to take part in some project because their advice is not heeded. Proud people cannot adjust without considerable embarrassment to unplanned or unexpected happenings.

Clowns teach us that the best therapy is a genuine sense of humor. People need to laugh with others but more important, at themselves. This is what the clown hopes to accomplish.

St. Paul's philosophy was quite similar. "Let no one delude himself. If any one of you thinks he is wise in a worldly way, he had better become a fool. In that way he will really be wise, for the wisdom of this world is absurdity with God" *(1 Cor. 3:18,19).*

Jesus, too, experienced being considered a fool. When Pilate sent him to be judged by Herod, Jesus remained silent. He said not one word in his own defense. Herod was so annoyed at Jesus' silence that he treated him like a fool.

"Herod and his guards then treated him with contempt and insult, after which they put a magnificent robe on him and sent him back to Pilate" *(Lk. 23:11).*

The Apostle reminds us that if we are really disciples of Jesus, then "We are fools on Christ's account. Ah, but in Christ you are wise!" *(1 Cor. 4:10).*

Praying with the following Scriptures will help us laugh at ourselves and laugh with others.

Romans 12:15,16-"Rejoice with those who rejoice,

weep with those who weep. Have the same at-titude toward all . . . . ''

Romans 15:7-''Accept one another, then, as Christ accepted you, for the glory of God.''

ll Corinthians 11:19,20-''Being wise yourselves, you gladly put up with fools. You even put up with those who exploit you . . . ''

Sirach 3:17,18-''My son, conduct your affairs with humility, and you will be loved more than a giver of gifts. Humble yourself the more, the greater you are, and you will find favor with God.''

l Peter 4:14-''Happy are you when you are insulted for the sake of Christ, for then God's Spirit in its glory has come to rest on you.''

l Corinthians 1:25-''For God's folly is wiser than men, and his weakness more powerful than men.''

Proverbs 14:16-''The wise man is cautious and shuns evil; the fool is reckless and sure of himself.''

17

RAIN IN DUE SEASON

I visited a young priest, a victim of cancer, on his deathbed. I asked him what I could do for him. At first his request startled me.

Since he was already too weak to leave his bed, he asked me to walk in the rain with my face lifted up so that I might feel every drop as it touched my skin. This young priest liked rain. He enjoyed it falling on his face. It reminded him of the gentle, fruitful outpouring of God's gifts upon us every moment of every day.

How often I take the rain for granted! How frequently I complain about the rain and the inconveniences of carrying an umbrella or wearing a raincoat or even cancelling plans for some outdoor work or recreation.

How generously God waters our thirsty earth! How providently he supplies this absolute necessity of life. How easily I forget! How often I turn on the faucet for a refreshing drink, or delight in an invigorating shower with no thought of gratitude to a provident Father!

The psalmist reminds us of God's goodness: ''. . . it rained from heaven at the presence of God, . . . A bountiful rain you showered down, O God, upon your inheritance; you restored the land when it languished'' *(Ps. 68:9,10).*

The coming of Jesus into the world is foretold by the prophet as a nourishing rain. "He shall be like rain coming down on the meadow, like showers watering the earth" *(Ps. 72:6).*

A person once asked me how she could become more and more aware of God's presence in her life. I suggested that the next day she should take an "awareness walk" in order to see God's creative, sustaining power in everything she would see along the way: in the chirping of the birds, in the singular beauty of each flower, in each tree, in every blade of grass.

The next day the rain fell relentlessly without even a momentary interruption. When this person returned the next evening, she informed me that her nose was a little flatter from pushing against the window pane, but that she must have said a million "thank you's" as she tried to count each raindrop as a blessing.

A song of former years reminds us: "April showers bring May flowers." May these same showers nurture grateful hearts and may God's Word keep us ever mindful of his providential care and concern for our welfare.

Isaiah 45:8-"Let justice descend, O heavens, like dew from above, like gentle rain let the skies drop it down . . . ."

Leviticus 26:4-"I will give you rain in due season, so that the land will bear its crops, and the trees their fruit;"

Psalm 65:10-"You have visited the land and watered it; greatly have you enriched it . . . ."

Zechariah 10:1-"Ask of the Lord rain in the spring season! It is the Lord who makes the storm clouds, and sends men the pouring rain; for everyone, grassy fields."

Sirach 43:23-"The dripping clouds restore them all, and the scattered dew enriches the parched land."

Acts 14:17-"Yet in bestowing his benefits, he has not hidden himself completely, without a clue. From the heavens he sends down rain and rich harvests; your spirits he fills with food and delight."

Isaiah 30:23-"He will give rain for the seed that you sow in the ground, and the wheat that the soil produces will be rich and abundant. . . ."

18

FRIEND OR FOE

Each day I try to find God in the ordinary happenings of the day. I do not try to program God, nor as a rule do I select a special theme for the day. I just let happen what may.

A few days ago I made a brief business trip to a little town not many miles from home. After I had passed the city limits by several miles, I came upon a farmer burning the stubble off a large field which had already yielded its harvest. As the fire moved toward the center of the field, it appeared like a blazing halo—a beautiful sight to behold.

I thought of the many blessings of fire as one of God's great gifts when used as intended by its Creator. As I was enjoying this reflection, I came upon another scene a few miles down the highway which evidenced the disastrous effect of fire. A whole mountainside—hundreds of acres—was burned off during the dry summer months. The charred tree trunks, standing like black ghosts, gave witness to the devouring menace which fire can be. Like an immense vulture it had not only consumed the beauty of God's creation, but had also wasted his gifts of valuable timber.

On the other hand, fire is a gracious gift from God when used as divinely intended, as it supplies warmth and heat. I recalled the many happy evenings spent around a campfire which not only served us in preparing delectable meals, but also served as the focal point for our evenings of sharing and singing.

I could also visualize another campfire on the shore of the Sea of Galilee. This charcoal fire helped Jesus prepare a picnic breakfast for his apostles after they had spent a fruitless night of fishing. "When they landed, they saw a charcoal fire there with a fish laid on it. . ." (Jn. 21:9).

Fire is one of God's many blessings. However, like any of God's gifts, fire can be abused. Many lives have been lost in some deadly inferno caused by carelessness or neglect. What destruction has been wrought by a disturbed arsonist!

The symbolism of fire is used by St. James in

speaking of our gift of speech. It, too, can be abused. The Apostle would have us heed the misuse of the tongue when he compares it to a devastating fire: "...See how tiny the spark is that sets a huge forest ablaze! The tongue is such a flame" (Jas. 3:5,6).

We often speak of love as a consuming fire burning within us. God's love is a purifying fire melting away the dross and keeping our focus on him.

The Word of the Lord also has the power of fire. When Jesus explained the Scripture to the two disciples on the way to Emmaus, they later admitted: "...Were not our hearts burning inside us as he talked to us on the road and explained the Scriptures to us?" (Lk. 24:32).

May his Word keep our hearts burning within us as we listen attentively and quietly.

Luke 12:49-"I have come to light a fire on the earth. How I wish the blaze were ignited!"

Acts 2:3, 4-"Tongues as of fire appeared which parted and came to rest on each of them. All were filled with the Holy Spirit...."

Hebrews 12:29-"...For our God is a consuming fire."

Luke 24:32-"...Were not our hearts burning inside us as he talked to us on the road and explained the Scriptures to us?"

I Peter 4:12, 13-"Do not be surprised, beloved, that a trial by fire is occurring in your midst. It is a test for you, but it should not catch you off guard. Rejoice instead, in the measure that you share Christ's sufferings...."

Acts 28:2-"The natives showed us extraordinary kindness by lighting a fire and gathering us all around it, for it had begun to rain and was growing cold."

I Corinthians 3:13-"the work of each will be made clear. The Day will disclose it. That Day will make its appearance with fire, and fire will test the quality of each man's work."

19

HANDS HELD ALOFT

Have you ever prayed with your arms extended in the form of a cross? If you timed yourself while praying in this position, you were probably surprised to discover how brief was the time you spent in prayer in that position.

Such an experience gives us a better appreciation of the Israelites in the desert. Joshua was engaged in battle with their enemies, the Amalekites. Moses went to the top of a hill to pray. As long as he kept his arms raised in prayer, the Israelites succeeded in battle. As soon as he rested his hands, Amalek had the better of the fight. It was then that Aaron and Hur supported his arms until sunset and the battle was won *(Ex. 17:8–13).*

Even though his arms were supported by Aaron and Hur, Moses still must have endured great physical pain as he maintained his prayer posture. His aching muscles must have cried out for relief. Physical pain, cheerfully and willingly accepted, is one kind of penance.

I love that story because it reminds us that penance helps our prayer. When we pray with our arms outstretched, we offer our prayer to God with one hand, with the other our willingness to give, especially our own wills. Did you ever notice how frequently the combination of the words, 'prayer and penance', are used to express an appropriate attitude before God?

St. Paul also mentions these characteristics of prayer. He says: "It is my wish, then, that in every place the men shall offer prayers with blameless hands held aloft and be free from anger and dissension *(I Tim. 2:8).*

St. Paul is speaking here of another kind of penance which is a condition for prayer. "To be free from anger and dissension" means a dying to self on many occasions. It means that we must forgive injury; we must accept the pain of being misunderstood; we must be willing to suffer persecution and, above all, we must continue to love. All this is mortification. All these we offer with the hand of penance.

Jesus also emphasized the necessity of penance along with prayer. On one occasion when his disciples were unable to expel the evil spirit from a young lad, Jesus said: "This kind does not leave but by prayer and fasting" (Mt. 17:21).

On the cross with his two hands extended in prayer, Jesus made the supreme oblation of himself to his Father. In the words of the psalmist he prayed: "Father, into your hands I commend my spirit" (Lk. 23:46). This was the total gift of himself in love. As we raise our two hands in prayer and penance, may our interior disposition be gracious and generous, trusting and confident.

In the Book of Psalms we find this prayer-posture mentioned frequently. Let us pray with the psalmist.

Psalm 28:2-"Hear the sound of my pleading, when I cry to you, lifting up my hands toward your holy shrine."

Psalm 63:5-"Thus will I bless you while I live; lifting up my hands, I will call upon your name."

Psalm 31:6-"Into your hands I commend my spirit; you will redeem me, O Lord, O faithful God."

Psalm 47:2-"All you peoples clap your hands, shout to God with cries of gladness."

Psalm 88:10-". . . daily I call upon you, O Lord; to you I stretch out my hands."

Psalm 119:48-". . . I will lift up my hands to your commands and meditate on your statutes."

Psalm 143:6-"I stretch out my hands to you; my soul thirsts for you like parched land."

20

DOWN THE BANNISTER

I arrived for a meeting at a school just as classes were being dismissed for the day. Needless to say, the students were a happy lot with another day of classes over. They were "free" once again.

The stairway leading up from the front entrance to the first-floor hallway had a wide, hardwood, highly polished bannister. The temptation was too great.

Some of the boys were releasing some of their pent-up energy by sliding down the bannister. Some were real experts, while others were less proficient. If a boy would happen to slide off the bannister before reaching the bottom, his companions would rate him a failure with a resounding "You flunked!" This procedure went on, with only those boys who had successfully reached the bottom permitted to compete. The sole survivor was the champion of the day.

This performance brought to my mind a certain dedicated person who loves God intensely. One day she told me that every time she seemed to be making some progress in her spiritual growth and had succeeded in climbing one step higher up the ladder of sanctity, she invariably would slide down the bannister to begin the process all over again.

Does this sound like a familiar refrain? If so, join the rest of us wayfarers. How often we thought that we might be making a little progress in our spiritual maturation, only to discover that down the bannister we would come sailing with incredible speed.

If this has ever happened to you, be assured that you are in good company. How St. Paul lamented this weakness in himself:

"I cannot understand my own actions. I do not what I want to do, but what I hate. The desire to do right is there but not the power. What happens is that I do, not the good I will to do, but the evil I do not intend. What a wretched man I am! Who can free me from this body under the power of death?" (Rom. 7:15-24)

After admitting his own weakness, St. Paul found hope and reassurance when he recognized that only the Lord can give the gift and power to live according to his way. When St. Paul came to this realization, his heart rejoiced: "All praise to God, through Jesus Christ, our Lord!" *(Rom. 7:25).*

We have even more reassurance. God does not judge the success or failure of our endeavors as we do. He looks only at our intentions and the extent to which we are striving to translate our love into action. If we want to love God, he accepts it as our love regardless of how imperfect it may be. If we could love God perfectly, he would have to give us the power and the gift to do so. The same is true of all our efforts in life.

The all-important question is: Do we want to? Success depends not on how high we ascend, but rather on how great is our desire and our determination to want to climb.

As we prayerfully listen to what the Lord is saying

to us in his Word, the answer will come in the quiet of our own heart.

Sirach 1:19–21-"One cannot justify unjust anger; anger plunges a man to his downfall. A patient man need stand firm but for a time, and then contentment comes back to him. For a while he holds back his words, then the lips of many herald his wisdom."

Job 11:13–15-"If you set your heart aright and stretch out your hands toward him, if you remove all iniquity from your conduct, and let not injustice dwell in your tent, surely then you may lift up your face in innocence; you may stand firm and unafraid."

Psalm 27:1–5-". . . The Lord is my life's refuge;. . . . For he will hide me in his abode in the day of trouble;. . . he will set me high upon a rock."

II Corinthians 12:9-". . . My grace is enough for you, for in weakness power reaches perfection."

Galatians 6:9-"Let us not grow weary of doing good; if we do not relax our efforts, in due time we shall reap our harvest."

Philippians 3:12, 13-". . . I give no thought to what lies behind but push on to what is ahead."

I John 1:8, 9-"If we say, 'We are free of the guilt of sin,' we deceive ourselves; the truth is not to be found in us. But if we acknowledge our sins, he who is just can be trusted to forgive our sins and cleanse us from every wrong.''

21

LIKE A SPONGE

Washing a car is not my most cherished pastime, nor my favorite form of recreation. However, my vanity and budget pressure me into this chore from time to time.

Recently, as I was preparing to wash my car, I dropped a dry sponge into a pail of water. Almost instantly the thirsty sponge had absorbed its full capacity of water. As the gurgling of the air bubbles quieted down, a thought struck me and started me off on a rambling reflection.

I am like a dry sponge. Jesus is the source of living water. He wants to fill me with himself. He penetrates my whole being. I am totally immersed in him, saturated by him as the sponge in the water.

These thoughts carried me to the image of the expansive ocean. If a tiny sponge were tossed into the ocean, it could never begin to absorb the limitless supply of water contained in the immense ocean. The thought staggers our imagination.

Yet, that mighty ocean is dwarfed by the infinity of the ocean of God's love which envelops and fills us. How comforting the brief statement of St. Luke:

"In him we live and move and have our being, . . . "(Acts 17:28).

A fable is told of a little fish who asked his mother, "what is this water I hear so much about?" The mother laughed as she informed him that he was swimming about in it, that he was buoyed up by it and that his life was sustained by it as he breathed it in.

For those of us who survive only on God's gift of oxygen a similar fable is told of a little cub-bear. He asked his mother, "What is this atmosphere we hear so much about?" Mother-bear's response was much the same as mother-fish's answer, "You silly thing, the atmosphere of which you have been hearing is surrounding you at every moment. You are bathed in it at this very instant. As you breathe in this atmosphere, it keeps you alive."

Fables, yes, but what apt reminders that we, too, live because of God's great love for us. We are baptized into the trinitarian life and love. We are the temples of the Holy Spirit, who is the fullness of Jesus dwelling in us as in his temple. This gives us our real dignity as Christians.

Jesus promised: "I will ask the Father and he will give you another Paraclete to be with you always . . . you can recognize him because he remains with you and . . . within you" (Jn. 14:16–17).

And our loving Father promised: "I will dwell with them and walk among them. I will be their God and they shall be my people . . . I will welcome you and be a father to you, and you will be my sons and daughters"(II Cor. 6:16–18).

What greater Gift can there be! But I must get on with washing my car. Today I finished this chore with greater alacrity than ever before.

As the little fish, and the cub-bear we, too, live, move and have our being in the presence of the Lord who is with us and within us. May this awareness come to us with greater intensity as we ponder his Word.

Galatians 4:6-"The proof that you are sons is the fact that God has sent forth into our hearts the spirit of his Son which cries out, "Abba!" ('Father!')."

John 14: 16, 17 -"I will ask the Father and he will give you another Paraclete...he remains with you and will be within you."

I Corinthians 3:16-"Are you not aware that you are the temple of God, and that the Spirit of God dwells in you?"

Galatians 2:20-"...the life I live now is not my own; Christ is living in me."

John 15:1-8-"I am the vine, you are the branches. He who lives in me and I in him, will produce abundantly, ..."

Matthew 28:20-"...know that I am with you always, until the end of the world!"

Psalm 95:5-"His is the sea, for he has made it, and the dry land, which his hands have formed."

22

HE SPRINKLES THE SNOW

A friend of ours was visiting recently from the state of Hawaii. Never in her life had she ever seen snow falling. She was so anxious to witness the sight of falling snow.

God was good enough to oblige, for "He sprinkles the snow like fluttering birds" *(Sir. 43:18).* During her brief sojourn with us, it did snow lightly. Our guest was in ecstasy. She wanted to cry out to the world that it was snowing beautiful white fluffy snow.

She went out of doors to be in the snow. She held her head aloft so that the delicate flakes could touch her face as they fell ever so gently. She wore black gloves as she caught some flakes in her hand. She was amazed at the artistry and delicacy of each individual flake. Each one was so intricate and unique. She was simply overcome with awe and amazement.

We enjoyed her exuberance and rejoiced with her. However, most of us were tired of shovelling snow by this time of the year, and some of us had experienced slipping and sliding as well as getting stuck in the snow.

Nevertheless, in her enthusiasm our guest brought me to a new appreciation of God's infinite goodness. The snow reminded me of how caringly God covered the earth to protect it against the cold harsh winter. I realized once again how much moisture snow brings to our parched earth. Likewise the snow packed in the mountains assures us of a steady water supply during the hot summer months. Nor can we pass by all the winter games, sledding, skiing, skating, which are enjoyed by adults as well as by children.

All these blessings I take so much for granted. Sometimes I fail to admire how artistically God decorates the trees, shrubs and even our homes with the pure white blanket. He makes our area a winter wonderland. As the psalmist admonishes us, we need to be still to appreciate more deeply God's handiwork.

As I enjoyed our guest's exuberance, I, too, caught some snowflakes in my hand to admire the intricate formation and lacy pattern of each tiny flake. I had forgotten momentarily the creative genius of God, reflected in each snowflake.

The Lord arrests our attention when he compares the inherent power of rain and snow to the transforming power of his Word:

"For just as from the heavens the rain and snow come down and do not return there till they have watered the earth, making it fertile and fruitful . . . So shall my word be that goes forth from my mouth; It shall not return to me void, but shall do my will, achieving the end for which I sent it" (Is. 55:10, 11).

Using his Word as the basis of our prayer each day will bring us to a richer appreciation of God's creative love. May the suggested texts which follow speak to your heart.

Daniel 3:70-"Ice and snow, bless the Lord; praise and exalt him above all forever."

Proverbs 26:1-"Like snow in summer, or rain in harvest, honor for a fool is out of place."

Sirach 43:18–20-"He sprinkles the snow like fluttering birds; it comes to settle like swarms of locusts. Its shining whiteness blinds the eyes, the mind is baffled by its steady fall. He scatters frost like so much salt; it shines like blossoms on the thornbush."

John 15:4-"Live on in me, as I do in you. No more than a branch can bear fruit of itself apart from the vine, can you bear fruit apart from me."

Psalm 51:9-". . . wash me and I shall be whiter than snow . . ."

Isaiah 1:18-". . . Though your sins be like scarlet, they may become white as snow; though they be crimson red, they may become white as wool."

Psalm 148:7,8-"Praise the Lord from the earth, . . . Fire and hail, snow and mist, storm winds that fulfill his word;"

23

INTANGIBLE PRESENCE

There are many and various presences in our lives. There is something unique and mysterious about the different ways we are present to one another. Sometimes we are consciously and physically present to one another. Other times we are in the immediate physical proximity of another person without, however, being aware of his or her presence. Our long distance phone calls make us very present to one another even though miles separate us.

The bishops of the Second Vatican Council tell us that "He (Jesus) is present in the sacrifice of the Mass...By His power He is present in the sacraments...He is present in His Word, since it is He Himself who speaks when the holy Scriptures are read in the Church..." *(Const. on Liturgy #7).*

In our home we try to keep ourselves aware that Jesus is very much present in his Word as recorded in the Bible.

We have a little shrine on which the Bible is enthroned, the open pages reflecting our openness to his Word. At times a flickering candle keeps vigil and reminds us that Jesus is the light of the world. Frequently a little flower adds its beauty to our shrine, but it also reminds us that He is creator and provider, Lord and Master of the universe. The flower also reminds us that he is always smiling upon us. Is not a flower the smile of God?

Jesus speaks to us through his Word. We need to be open and receptive to his Word. Listening is difficult in our age of noise, speed and confusion. Silence and solitude are essential for listening to his Word with our whole being.

Jesus explained very simply, but very clearly, the power of his Word if we listen and keep his Word. In his own inimitable way, Jesus teaches us a precious lesson about hearing his Word when he told us the parable of the sower going out to sow his seed. Some fell on the footpath, some among thorns, some among the rocks and some on good ground.

At the insistence of the apostles, Jesus explained the four classes of persons who hear the Word, and the harvest which it brings forth in their lives. Listen to Jesus as he explains this parable *(Mt. 13:4–23)*.

On another occasion, Jesus explained that his Mother's true greatness was not so much that she gave birth to him physically, but rather that she listened to the Word of God and permitted it to become the source of direction and inspiration in her life.

How powerful are his words! "Rather, blest are they who hear the word of God and keep it" *(Lk. 11:27, 28)*.

John 14:18–20-"On that day you will know that I am in my Father and you in me, and I in you."

I John 3:24-"And this is how we know that he remains in us: from the Spirit that he gave us."

l John 4:16-"God is love, and he who abides in love abides in God, and God in him."

John l:14-"The Word became flesh and made his dwelling among us . . ."

Revelation 21:3-"He shall dwell with them and they shall be his people and he shall be their God who is always with them."

ll Corinthians 6:16-"I will dwell with them and walk among them . . ."

Galatians 2:20-". . .the life I live now is not my own; Christ is living in me."

24

DINNER WITH THE MURPHYS

My dinner with the Murphy family was a much different experience than I had anticipated. I was fed sumptuously—not only physically, but spiritually as well.

When I arrived, I could see from the driveway six newly-washed little faces watching eagerly for my coming. Seldom have I ever enjoyed such an exciting and warm welcoming committee. It was a delight.

That evening they gave me very much to think about, and I still ponder it with joy. In the first place, the parents let the children be themselves. They did not demand any unusual or unnatural deportment from the children because I was there. This made me feel very much at home. The only major problem arose when we were to be seated at table. I could not sit next to six children all at the same time.

When we got seated, the father told me that they had a family custom to let each person have an opportunity to say a little prayer or read a short scriptural text or share some incident of the day in which it was quite apparent that God was playing a major role.

The four-year old prayed that her friend, Mary Ann, could run as fast as she, herself, could run. I was amused at this petition concluding that this prayer sprang from our awareness of joggers and marathons. Only later, I was surprised to learn that Mary Ann was a little spastic child living next door who had never walked a step in her life.

Another child thanked God for Daddy who had earned enough money to buy food and for Mother who had prepared it with a special mention for eight-year old Cecile who had peeled the potatoes.

Joe, age 12, shared that he knew God wanted them to win their softball game that afternoon, especially since he, himself, got four hits and drove in three runs.

Mother thanked God for the good health and love of all of her children, to which a little one responded: "God, I love you almost as much as I love Daddy."

When it was my turn, I was so moved that all I could stammer was, "Thank you, Lord, for all the Murphys."

I did not quite understand whether the baby was responding with Amens or Alleluias as she "Ah-ed, Ah-ed, Ah-ed" her contribution to the family prayer.

After a delicious and inspiring meal, I was asked to say the closing prayer. St. Paul came to my rescue as I reached for my little pocket-size New Testament. This I borrowed directly from him:

> "We keep thanking God for all of you and we remember you in our prayers, for we constantly are mindful before our God and Father of the way you are proving your faith, and laboring in love, and showing constancy of hope in our Lord Jesus Christ"
> (I Thes. 1:2,3).

Eating at the table of the Lord's Word supplies such abundant nourishment "so that the man of God may be fully competent and equipped for every good work" (II Tim. 3:17).

Revelation 3:20-"Here I stand, knocking at the door. If anyone hears me calling and opens the door, I will enter his house and have supper with him, and he with me."

Luke 22:14,15-"When the hour arrived, he took his place at table, and the apostles with him. He said to them: 'I have greatly desired to eat this Passover with you before I suffer.' "

I Peter 4:8,9-"Above all, let your love for one

another be constant, for love covers a multitude of sins. Be mutually hospitable without complaining."

Psalm 128:3-"Your wife shall be like a fruitful vine in the recesses of your home; your children like olive plants around your table."

Hebrews 13:1,2-"Love your fellow Christians always. Do not neglect to show hospitality, for by that means some have entertained angels without knowing it."

Mark 10:14-"Let the children come to me and do not hinder them. It is to just such as these that the kingdom of God belongs."

I Peter 4:10-"As generous distributors of God's manifold grace, put your gifts at the service of one another, each in the measure he has received."

25

TRAPPED

Across the street from where I was staying stood an old unoccupied apartment house. The shutters were closed, the doors and windows securely barred and bolted. One day a young couple came to inspect the second floor apartment. They opened everything up wide to give it a much-needed ventilating.

Before leaving they closed it up tight again: windows, doors, shutters. Only one small window above the door leading to the balcony was left unshuttered. As I glanced toward the house, I saw a small bird trapped inside. It flew and fluttered against that unshuttered window pane above the door. The bird flew in panic against the glass, searching for an escape route.

The second day the bird continued to flutter against the glass, but its sorties were less frequent and less vigorous. Apparently its strength was waning.

I tried to the find the owner of the building but without success. The neighbors had no knowledge of his identity, nor any key. The bird seemed hopelessly trapped to await its death.

Later that day as I was trying to spend time in prayer, a terrible anger welled up within me. It was a long-standing anger toward a certain person whom I had not seen for months. Many times, as I prayed for a healing, the anger seemed to subside, only to be inflamed again for no apparent reason. I tried to rid myself of this anger but with little success.

I am like that imprisoned bird. I am held captive. My own anger holds me bound. Like the little bird, I have tried various escapes, but the feeling persists from time to time.

Again my thoughts went back to the little bird. If the house could have been opened wide, the little bird could have flown away to food, freedom and safety.

Like my feathered friend, I am not free, but

restricted by my anger. Only Jesus holds the key. Only he can help me. Only he can free me. Jesus came into the world as our healer. He heals in every conceivable area because he loves. His love compels him to reach out to those imprisoned and to the suffering. "Jesus Christ is the same yesterday, today and forever"(Heb. 13:7). He wants to heal as much today as in those days when he walked the face of the earth.

His invitation is always the same, to the end of time: "Come to me, all you who are weary and find life burdensome, and I will refresh you" (Mt. 11:28).

Again he assures us how much he wants to come to us to free us with his healing love. "Here I stand, knocking at the door. If anyone hears me calling and opens the door, I will enter his house and have supper with him, and he with me" (Rev. 3:20). Jesus would gently remind us that the latchstring is on the inside; we must open to him.

My heart ached for the little bird, but I am grateful to God for the spiritual insight it gave me.

When we feel we are held captive by some human weakness or some exterior force, we will find great healing and freedom in his Word.

Isaiah 42:6,7-"I, the Lord have called you. . . To open the eyes of the blind, to bring out prisoners from confinement, and from the dungeon, those who live in darkness."

Matthew 25:36-". . . I was ill and you comforted me, in prison and you came to visit me."

Psalm 142:8—"Lead me forth from prison, that I may give thanks to your name...."

John 11:44-"...'Untie him,' Jesus told them, 'and let him go free.'"

II Timothy 1:8-"Therefore, never be ashamed of your testimony to our Lord, nor of me, a prisoner for his sake; but with the strength which comes from God bear your share of the hardship which the gospel entails."

Ephesians 4:1,2-"I plead with you, then, as a prisoner for the Lord, to live a life worthy of the calling you have received, with perfect humility, meekness, and patience, bearing with one another lovingly."

26

SHIFTING SAND

I was enjoying a contemplative walk along a path in the desert. The sand was well packed by the relentless beating of the wind. It afforded some solid footing as I walked along.

In the afternoon a gentle breeze gusted into a strong wind. I decided to return to the shelter of my hermitage. The wind became so violent that it blew clouds of sand and dust high enough to obscure the sun. The wind-driven sand began to drift in various places.

As I was retracing my steps over the same path by which I had travelled a short time before, I found it difficult to find the path. In some places it had been completely obliterated by the shifting sand. Walking in the soft, swirling sand became extremely difficult and exhausting.

With my head bent low to protect my face from the stinging sand, I reflected on the sand which I permit to come into my own interior life. That sand impedes my progress on my spiritual pilgrimage to the Father.

The sand takes on many forms. It can be my tenacity in clinging to my own opinions, my self-centeredness, my many and various attachments which cause me to lose my focus on my final destiny. Like the desert sand these are so fickle and changeable. Like the desert sand they mount into a cloud, obscuring my vision of God who must be my first priority.

Jesus warned us about building our hopes and dreams on sand. He said: "Anyone who hears my words but does not put them into practice is like the foolish man who built his house on sandy ground. The rains fell, the torrents came, the winds blew and lashed against his house. It collapsed under all this and was completely ruined"(Mt. 7:26,27).

We know the dangers and havoc which can be caused by flash floods in the desert. As we journey along life's highway, we are repeatedly warned about the dangers which torrential rains pose. On my inner journey the same cautions and warnings are flashing if I am attentive to them.

On the other hand Jesus assures us: "Anyone who hears my words and puts them into practice is like the wise man who built his house on rock. When the rainy season set in, the torrents came and the winds blew and buffeted his house. It did not collapse; it had been solidly set on rock" (Mt. 7:24,25).

Jesus promises that if we are true to his word: ". . . my Father will love him; we will come to him and make our dwelling place with him" (Jn. 14:23).

This reassurance makes our inner journey a real joy. His Word gives us this reassurance.

Hosea 2:16-". . . I will lead her into the desert and speak to her heart."

Wisdom 7:9-". . . all gold, in view of her (Wisdom), is a little sand, and before her, silver is to be accounted mire."

Colossians 3:2-"Be intent on things above rather than on things of earth."

Psalm 73:2,3-"But, as for me, I almost lost my balance; my feet all but slipped, because I was envious of the arrogant when I saw them prosper though they were wicked."

Galatians 1:6-"I am amazed that you are so soon deserting him who called you in accord with his gracious design in Christ, and are going over to another gospel."

Psalm 37:23,24-"By the Lord are the steps of man

made firm, and he approves his way. Though he
fall, he does not lie prostrate, for the hand of the
Lord sustains him."

Galatians 3:3-"How could you be so stupid? After
beginning in the spirit, are you now to end in the
flesh?"

27

WATERED GARDEN

I do not profess to be a horticulturist, nor have I
been blessed with a green thumb, but I do enjoy put-
tering around in my garden. Gardening often leads
me Godward.

As I patiently wait for the seed to germinate, watch
it grow into a plant, enjoy its blossoming and bearing fruit—I am very much aware of the presence of
God. His creative love is dynamic and operative in
every plant. The chemical process of germination,
growth and development is mysterious because it is
divine. Watching this process in my garden keeps
me close to the Giver of Life.

I do not think it is stretching the metaphor too far
to see my own spiritual growth and maturation as a
garden. Yes, I am like a garden in so many ways.

If the soil in a garden is dry and baked by the sun,

it becomes a hard shell. The seed cannot penetrate this hard crust and fails to germinate; it cannot expose itself to the warmth of the sun. No harvest is forthcoming.

I can very easily become like the soil in the garden. My self-centeredness often encloses me in a hard shell. Encased in this hard shell the Holy Spirit, dwelling within us as the source of love, cannot use me as a channel to radiate his love and peace to others. My insecurity keeps me on the defensive. I am reluctant to let others reach out to me. How much I need the softening water of God's healing love.

Water is essential. As a garden drinks in the soft rain or is watered regularly, growth not only flourishes; but the garden soon becomes an oasis, radiating the beauty of its Creator.

If I am to grow and mature spiritually, I need to be watered with the living water of God's divine life and love. Like the soil I must be conditioned and remain porous to receive the gentle rain of his love.

The prophet reminds us of God's living water:

"He will renew your strength, and you shall be like a watered garden, like the spring whose water never fails" (Is. 58:11).

When I reach out in love to others and share God's love with them, he will continue to fill me with an abundance of his love. The more I give it away the more will come to me. Then I will be "like the spring whose water never fails."

Using the image of living water, Jesus makes a gigantic leap from natural water to supernatural life.

He tried to explain to the Samaritan woman his indwelling as living water. With the Samaritan woman, let us plead: "Give me this water, sir, so that I shall not grow thirsty..." (Jn. 4:15).

His word is the inexhaustible fountain of living water as we contemplate its message to us.

Isaiah 44:3-"I will pour out water upon the thirsty ground, and streams upon the dry land;..."

John 4:10–15-"...the water I give shall become a fountain within him leaping up to provide eternal life."

Sirach 39:16,17-"The works of God are all of them good; in its own time every need is supplied. At his word the waters become still as in a flask; he had but to speak and the reservoirs were made."

Revelation 2:7-"...I will see to it that the victor eats from the tree of life which grows in the garden of God!"

Psalm 65:10-"You have visited the land and watered it; greatly have you enriched it. God's watercourses are filled; you have prepared the grain."

Ezekiel 47:12-"Along both banks of the river, fruit trees of every kind shall grow; their leaves shall not fade, nor their fruit fail...."

Job 8:16-"He is full of sap before sunrise, and beyond his garden his shoots go forth."

28

POETRY IN A STORM

As I was driving home on the Interstate, I could see that I was heading right into a violent electrical storm. The black clouds were rolling their somber blanket over the landscape. The gusting winds were so strong that they rocked the car. The lightning flashed and the peals of thunder reverberated so loudly that they shattered the stillness of the evening twilight.

I found a rest stop along the highway and decided to drive in and wait out the storm. Besides, I enjoy watching the lightning and listening to the thunder.

I am grateful to my parents for more than I could ever recall. One lesson my mother taught me was never to fear a storm. She ingrained in me that God was taking care of me at every moment and since a storm was of his making, I should enjoy it rather than fear it. Throughout the years I have appreciated this wholesome admonition.

From my childhood days I also recall that someone was trying to allay my fear of a storm by telling me that the angels were laughing and rejoicing as they went about the duties of each day. The thunder we heard was the echo of their merry-making. In the same vein I was told that lightning was God's method of illuminating our way on a dark stormy night. In my gullible childhood, I accepted these tales without reservation. They did serve a purpose, however, of warding off any fear I would have of an electrical storm.

As I waited for the storm to subside, my thoughts turned to the storm which the apostles encountered when, on one occasion, they were trying to cross the Sea of Galilee. Jesus was asleep in the stern of the boat. When they cried out begging his help, he calmed the sea by a simple command: "Quiet! Be still!" *(Mk. 4:35–39)*. On another occasion, Jesus manifested his power over the winds and waves by walking on the water. When I recalled how he saved Peter who tried to walk on the water, he gave me the reassurance that he would likewise save me in the midst of any raging storm *(Mt. 14:22–31)*.

Many times the psalmist envisions our loving Father coming to our rescue by using the image of a storm. How poetically he describes the fury of a storm, be it a danger or threat of any nature whatsoever. He always assures us that God will come to our rescue, and with his help we will always be victorious.

Jesus gave us the same reassurance many times in the Gospel. He bids us: "Do not be afraid . . . Fear is useless . . . Fear not . . ." etc. Someone reminded me that the words "Fear not "or a similar expression is used 366 times in the Scriptures. This means one for each day of the year and an extra one for leap year.

In due time, the storm subsided and I continued my journey homeward with renewed awareness of the presence of the Lord at all times.

Listen with all your heart as the Lord continues to assure us of his loving protection.

Psalm 107:29-"He hushed the storm to a gentle breeze, and the billows of the sea were stilled. . . . "

Mark 10:49-"You have nothing to fear from him!"

Luke 8:50-"Fear is useless; what is needed is trust. . . "

Psalm 56:2–14-"In God, in whose promise I glory, in God I trust without fear. . . . "

Luke 12:32-"Do not live in fear, little flock. . . . "

Psalm 18:1–15-"He inclined the heavens and came down. . . . "

l John 4:18-"Love has no room for fear; rather, perfect love casts out all fear."

29

DE-FEATHER BEDDING

I am always fascinated by the legends and lore which comes out of the culture of our native Americans. There is so much deep spiritual significance contained in it.

When one of my Indian friends was making a retreat, he shared with me something of the habits of the eagle. When an eagle builds its nest high above God's earth, it fills the bottom of the nest with hard, sharp objects. These in turn are covered with feathers and softer material. The eagle then lays her eggs on the soft bedding. When the young eagles break through their shells, they rest on this soft downy bed.

However, when it is time for the young to leave their nest, all the soft material is gradually thrown out of the nest. All that remains is the hard, sharp objects which are by no means comfortable. This forces the young eagles to leave their nest and seek their fortunes in the world.

Our heavenly Father follows a similar pattern in nurturing us in the sunshine of his love, molding us, shaping us and transforming us. In his Song to the whole assembly of Israel, Moses used this same image to remind them of God's providential care of them:

"As an eagle incites its nestlings forth by hovering over its brood, so he spread his wings to receive them and bore them up on his pinions" *(Deut. 32:11).*

When we are ready, Jesus calls us forth into varied ministries. He first bids us: "Come and see," then only "Follow me" *(Jn. 1:39, 43).* Next he commissions us: "Go into the whole world and proclaim the good news to all creation" *(Mk. 16:15).*

Jesus does not trick us into following him. He does not offer us much of the world's comforts, but rather he points to his own life. "The foxes have lairs, the birds in the sky have nests, but the Son of Man has nowhere to lay his head" *(Mt. 8:20).*

Furthermore, Jesus never asks us to do anything which he, himself, has not already experienced.

What loneliness, what fear and trepidation Jesus must have felt when he left the peaceful confines of his home in Nazareth!

When we respond to the Lord's call to grow in holiness by following him and also by loving and serving others, we may do so with fear and some misgivings. However, we have the assurance that Jesus will not leave us in a vulnerable and unsupported position. Did he not say: "Know that I am with you always, until the end of the world" *(Mt. 28:20).*

The psalmist gives us the same reassurance:

"With his pinions he will cover you, and under his wings you shall take refuge"*(Ps. 91:4).*

Listening to some of the many reassurances which the Lord gives us will convince our hearts and minds.

Psalm 91:4-"With his pinions he will cover you, and under his wings you shall take refuge;"

Matthew 8:24–27-". . . 'Lord, save us! We are lost!' He said to them: 'Where is your courage? How little faith you have!. . .' "

John 16:20-"I tell you truly: you will weep and mourn while the world rejoices; you will grieve for a time, but your grief will be turned to joy."

Matthew 6:33-"Seek first his kingship over you, his way of holiness, and all these things will be given you besides."

James 5:7-"Be patient, therefore, my brothers, until the coming of the Lord. See how the farmer awaits the precious yield of the soil . . . ."

John 16:33-". . . You will suffer in the world. But take courage! I have overcome the world."

I Peter 1:6,7-"There is cause for rejoicing here. You may for a time have to suffer the distress of many trials; but this is so that your faith, which is more precious than the passing splendor of fire-tried gold, may by its genuineness lead to praise, glory, and honor when Jesus Christ appears."

30

DID JESUS HAVE A DOG

One day a little boy asked his mother if Jesus had a dog when he was a boy. The mother thought for a moment then replied: "Well, Son, Jesus was like other little boys in Nazareth, so I suppose he did have a dog."

Her son mulled over that for awhile, then came back to his mother with his own conclusion:

"Mother, I don't think that Jesus had a dog because there was no dog with him on Calvary."

Zing! That response sent vibrations throughout my whole being. It hit me at the core of my being! Yes, a dog is a loyal animal, I had to admit. I asked myself: Am I always that loyal? Am I as faithful and devoted as a dog is to its master?

Jesus often felt the pain of disloyalty, of infidelity, and even rejection. How often he was deserted and left alone!

When Jesus began his public ministry in his own town of Nazareth he was not only rejected, but an attempt was even made on his life. "They rose up and expelled him from the town, leading him to the brow of the hill on which it was built and intending to hurl him over the edge. But he went straight through their midst and walked away" (Lk. 4:29,30). There is no mention of a dog being with Jesus even though he was in his home village where we might expect a dog to be with him if he had one.

Recall how he had prepared his followers for the crowning gift of his ministry—himself in the Eucharist. When he promised them his Eucharistic presence, how did his followers react: "From this time on many of his disciples broke away and would not remain in his company any longer" (Jn. 6:66). What sorrow Jesus must have experienced at their leaving!

In the loneliness of that dreadful hour in Gethsemane, Jesus needed human comfort and consolation. He asked his special friends, his apostles, to support him in prayer, but they fell asleep, unaware of the sword which was piercing his heart.

When the soldiers arrived to arrest him, his companions of the last three years again failed him. How pathetic the record in Scripture: "Then all the disciples deserted him and fled" *(Mt.26:56)*. The litany could go on: rejected by his own people, deserted by his disciples, denied by a chosen apostle, betrayed by the kiss of a friend. Nowhere do we find a dog mentioned in Scripture. If so, he might have been with Jesus.

These reflections racing through my mind gave me reason to pause and examine my own life and attitude. How often I have been too busy to give Jesus time in prayer, listening to what he longs to tell me. How frequently I reneged on my commitment to serve him faithfully by keeping my life God-centered! How readily I become self-centered.

How many times I murmured and even complained aloud about the weight of my cross. All too frequently I went to others for comfort and help and ignored his invitation: "Come to me all you who are weary and find life burdensome and I will refresh you" *(Mt. 11:28)*.

These reflections have carried me far from the question whether or not Jesus had a dog. Maybe the lad's reasoning was right: if Jesus did have a dog he would have faithfully stood by Jesus when others failed him.

As we daily ponder the Word of the Lord, we will grow in love and loyalty.

Tobit 6:2-"When the boy left home, accompanied by the angel, the dog followed Tobiah out of the house and went with them."

John 19:25-"Near the cross of Jesus there stood his mother. . . ."

Matthew 15:21–28-" 'It is not right to take the food of sons and daughters and throw it to the dogs. . .' 'Please Lord,' she insisted , 'even the dogs eat the leavings that fall from their masters' tables.' "

Jude 1:21-"Persevere in God's love, and welcome the mercy of our Lord Jesus Christ which leads to life eternal."

Revelation 2:10-"Have no fear of the sufferings to come. . . . Remain faithful until death and I will give you the crown of life."

II Timothy 2:3-"Bear hardship along with me as a good soldier of Christ Jesus."

Matthew 26:40, 41-"So you could not stay awake with me for even an hour? Be on guard, and pray that you may not undergo the test. The spirit is willing but nature is weak."

31

BODY LANGUAGE

Early one morning I was standing on Main street in a distant city waiting for my friend to meet me and drive me to my destination. My attention was attracted to a scene across the street. I witnessed a sight which filled my heart with joy.

A man was making his way slowly down the street apparently on his way to work. As he walked, he greeted every person along the way. He often turned to greet someone in a business establishment who seemed to be waiting for his greeting.

I noticed that several motorists waved to him. If this man was not looking in their direction, other motorists tooted their horns to attract his attention. In return they received an enthusiastic, waving gesture of a greeting.

Our greeter was an out-going person, to say the least, and obviously a very happy person. There was something unique about his waving. He had no hands. Two hooks served as hands.

A policeman sauntered along on my side of the street. I asked him about our genial greeter. He informed me that the man had lost both of his hands in an accident, but that he was determined not to let that interfere with his being a happy person. Each day on his way to and from work, the man radiated the joyful acceptance of his handicap to others. As he accepted his handicap, he began reaching out to others. As the policeman moved along, he said: "That man has a mission all his own."

For this man it was a personal apostolate. He simply exuded joy, peace and happiness, regardless of his condition in life.

My driver arrived and as we drove along, I shared this experience. My friend was well aware of this man's mission and told me that he was to be seen every morning and evening going to or coming from work, in the cold of winter or the heat of summer, always in the same cheerful mood.

Then I mused about our own apostolate as Christians. We are called to be apostles of joy. We have the Good News that God loves us and that we are destined for eternal happiness with him. This is precisely why Jesus came: to bring us the Good News of God's creating, caring, healing, forgiving, enduring love. He said: "All this I tell you that my joy may be yours and your joy may be complete" (Jn. 15:11).

At the moment of our Baptism we became the temples of the Holy Spirit. Among the fruits which the Spirit produces within us are love, peace and joy. We are to be a joyous people. We are called to be apostles of joy.

First we must experience the joy of the Lord, then we will automatically radiate that joy to others. Listen to Paul's admonition to us: "Rejoice in the Lord always! I say it again. Rejoice! Everyone should see how unselfish you are. The Lord is near. Dismiss all anxiety from your minds. Present your needs to God in every form of prayer and in petitions full of gratitude. Then God's own peace, which is beyond all understanding, will stand guard over your hearts and minds, in Christ Jesus" (Phil. 4:4–7).

John 14:27–28-". . . my peace is my gift to you. . . ."

I Corinthians 13:4–7-"Love is patient; love is kind. . . ."

Luke 2:10-". . . I come to proclaim good news to

you—tidings of great joy to be shared by the whole people.''

John 15:11-*''All this I tell you that my joy may be yours and your joy may be complete.''*

Psalm 21:7-*''For you made him a blessing forever; you gladdened him with the joy of your presence.''*

John 16:20–22-*''. . . your hearts will rejoice with a joy no one can take from you.''*

Psalm 63:8-*''That you are my help, and in the shadow of your wings I shout for joy.''*

32

COFFEE

Early morning rising has some advantages, although there are times when a later sleep would be welcome and beneficial. Since I am the first to rise in the morning, I usually make a pot of coffee. I have discovered that coffee can put one into a prayerful disposition. With a cup of coffee in hand,

I find a quiet spot close to a window to enjoy the moment of solitude.

Coffee helps us to sit quietly and reflectively. It is a stimulant which brings us gently into a deeper awareness of a new day. It does not arouse us harshly. It invites us to "be still and know that I am God" *(Ps. 46:11) (Grail Translation)*.

Coffee reminds us of God's divine life surging through every fibre of our being. His divine life dwelling within us reminds us of our dignity as his adopted sons and daughters.

How refreshing are Paul's words: "All who are led by the Spirit of God are sons of God... The Spirit himself gives witness with our spirit that we are children of God.... *(Rom. 8:14–16)*.

Early morning coffee can be very soothing to a raw throat. Its warmth dispels the hoarseness of our voice. His divine life present within us heals the harshness of our voice when speaking to others. He speaks kindly through us to others.

In his pastoral concern Paul gives sound advice: "Never let evil talk pass your lips; say only the good things men need to hear, things that will really help them. Get rid of harsh words..." *(Eph. 4:29)*. Again he says: "let us profess the truth in love and grow to the full maturity in Christ" *(Eph. 4:15)*.

What a paradox! Even though coffee is a stimulant, it can bring us into a quiet contemplative mood. As we sit quietly, inhaling its pleasing aroma and slowly sipping it in early morning, we are easily moved into the presence of God.

Entering into quiet prayer with the Lord is like sipping fresh coffee. We take only a little sip at a time. When we come to prayer, we can comprehend only a tiny facet of our transcendent God. His infinity staggers our imagination. We can savor only a sip at a time. His immanent love is ever at work, fashioning our hands, our eyes, our ability to walk and talk.

How delightful is our God! Yes, even his gift of coffee helps bring us into a deeper union with him.

As we finish our coffee, it is fitting to pause and thank our gracious God for all those who grew, harvested and prepared the coffee beans, as well as those who transported it and delivered it to our door.

In addition to that cup of cold water given in his name, would not Jesus add 'whoever gives a cup of hot coffee in my name will not be without his reward'?

One of the following Scriptures may be a stepping stone into a deeper, more personal relationship with the Lord as you contemplatively sip your cup of coffee.

Psalm 17:15-"But I in justice shall behold your face; on waking, I shall be content in your presence."

Mark 6:31-"Come by yourselves to an out-of-the-way place and rest a little. . . ."

Psalm 16:9- ". . . my heart is glad and my soul rejoices, my body, too, abides in confidence;"

Romans 8:26,27-"The Spirit too helps us in our weakness, for we do not know how to pray as we ought;"

John 16:24-"Until now you have not asked for

anything in my name. Ask and you shall receive,
that your joy may be full.''

Romans 12:12-''Rejoice in hope, be patient under
trial, persevere in prayer.''

Psalm 37:7-''Leave it to the Lord,and wait for him;''

33

POWERLESS

A violent wind storm blew up. Winds gusted up to 55 miles per hour. The damage caused by the storm was extensive: trees were blown over, poles with their power lines were toppled over by the violence of the wind. The whole area was blacked out as a result of the storm.

As I sat in the dark with only a flickering flame of a candle striving feebly to dispel the darkness, I had time to ponder and reflect on man's helplessness. Even though we have made such gigantic strides in technology, we are still so powerless against the forces of nature.

As the hours wore on, my room became colder and more uncomfortable. Without electricity the furnace was not operating, so dependent are we on electrical power. Since our water is pumped up a steep incline, we were without water for drinking, cooking, washing, bathing. How fragile our life without electricity! Our refrigerator and deep freeze were clamoring for power so that they might accomplish the end for which they were made.

With facility I made the transition into our spiritual life. Just as we are so dependent on electricity for power, comfort, convenience and even for our entertainment through radio and television, so we are dependent on God for everything.

Our spiritual growth and maturation depends on God. How much we need his divine life surging through every fibre of our being. How helpless we are unless he is energizing our whole being. How incapable we are of reaching out in selfless love to others if the power of his love does not flow freely through us.

With simple directness Jesus said: "Apart from me you can do nothing." This is just another way of saying that with him we can do all things. Jesus invites us to stay plugged into him when he bids us: "Live on in me, as I do in you. No more than a branch can bear fruit of itself apart from the vine, can you bear fruit apart from me" (Jn. 15:4).

The storm continued. The darkness and cold could not rob the peace and joy which came from pondering his powerful words. Perhaps St. Paul reflected on God's power in a similar storm when he prayed: "To him whose power now at work in us can do immeasurably more than we ask or imagine—to him be glory in the church and in Christ Jesus through all generations, world without end. Amen" (Eph. 3:20, 21).

101

Meditation and reflection come more easily in the dark. I thank God for the storm and for the insights he gave me.

In the glow of candle-lit atmosphere his Word may penetrate more readily into the recesses of our hearts, producing and generating a new power supply to live each day in his love.

II Corinthians 12:10-"*Therefore I am content with weakness, with mistreatment, with distress, with persecutions and difficulties for the sake of Christ; for when I am powerless, it is then that I am strong.*"

Psalm 103:13–14-"*As a father has compassion on his children, so the Lord has compassion on those who fear him, for he knows how we are formed; he remembers that we are dust.*"

Acts 1:8-"*You will receive power when the Holy Spirit comes down on you; then you are to be my witnesses in Jerusalem, throughout Judea and Samaria, yes, even to the ends of the earth.*"

Philippians 4:19,20-"*My God in turn will supply your needs fully, in a way worthy of his magnificent riches in Christ Jesus. All glory to our God and Father for unending ages! Amen.*"

Romans 5:6-"*At the appointed time, when we were still powerless, Christ died for us godless men.*"

Acts 4:33-"*With power the apostles bore witness to*

*the resurrection of the Lord Jesus, and great respect
was paid to them all;''*

*Galatians 4:9-''Now that you have come to know
God—or rather, have been known by him—how
can you return to those powerless, worthless,
natural elements to which you seem willing to en-
slave yourselves once more?''*

34

STORMS AND SWELLS

During our sojourn at the beach, the sea seemed
to be furiously angry. Relentlessly, it tossed its
tumultuous waves against the shore and slashed at
all the man-made infringements upon its boundaries.
The swells grew mountainously high as they
plunged shoreward with a mighty surge and in rapid
succession. The frothing, foamy surf, usually so
mesmerizingly beautiful, now rode the crest of the
turbulent waves and splashed high into the atmosphere before cascading over the breakwater. It
appeared as if the surf was trying to escape the fury
of the powerful waves. The rip-tides slashing across
the troubled waters were an ominous sight to
behold.

This gigantic upheaval of the roaring sea made sailing and surfing impossible. The sea was so violent that even the most ardent swimmer could not be tempted to go near the raging water.

My companion and I sat comfortably nestled leeward at a safe distance on the shore. Our alcove was high enough to give us a commanding panoramic view of the ocean for miles around. As Stephen and I sat in utter amazement at the might and power of the sea and at the turmoil billowing before us, we began to share some reflections.

I volunteered that at times our life, like the sea, becomes so storm-tossed that we cast our anger, frustrations and disappointments in every direction. Like a rip-tide we may even vent our irascibility on some unsuspecting person who may happen to cross our path. Please God, that this may happen very seldom if at all.

As we watched the surging, tossing, tumultuous water heaving and plunging high upon the beach, my friend Stephen recalled that at its depth the ocean is calm, still and placid. The mountainous turbulence is only on the surface of the ocean. This movement serves a good purpose, preventing the water from becoming stagnant. The volcanic outbursts of the raging water do not originate from the depth of the ocean, but occur only on the surface.

As I pondered what Stephen was saying I experienced great relief and deep peace. So many times I become irritable, angry, disturbed or unkind. I feel so guilty about this. It teaches me poverty of spirit in accepting my humanness. Then I realize that I am much like the ocean. My disturbance is not deep-rooted.

Like the ocean I am calm in the depth of my being. The reason is quite obvious. I am the temple of the Holy Spirit who is dwelling in me. He is the source of love, peace and joy. He is dynamic and operative within me if I give him the freedom to transform me. Like the ocean I must go to the depth of my being to discover real peace. Then I realize that, like the ocean, the storm is only on the surface; and I feel less guilty.

Furthermore, just as the storm-tossed waves keep the ocean water fresh, so my failings serve a good purpose. They help me grow spiritually. Humbly recognizing my failings and weaknesses will assist me in the process of maturing spiritually. They help me "put on the new man" and permit the image of Jesus to be formed in me.

These selections from his Word will enable me to calm the storms in my life and help me radiate the peace and joy which the Lord gives me.

Psalm 104:3-"You have constructed your palace upon the waters. You make the clouds your chariot; you travel on the wings of the wind."

Romans 14:4-"Who are you to pass judgement on another's servant? His master alone can judge whether he stands or falls. And stand he will, for the Lord is able to make him stand."

Psalm 93:4-"More powerful than the roar of many waters, more powerful than the breakers of the sea—powerful on high is the Lord."

Romans 8:26-"The Spirit too helps us in our

weakness, for we do not know how to pray as we ought; but the Spirit himself makes intercession for us with groanings that cannot be expressed in speech.''

Psalm 16:8-''I set the Lord ever before me; with him at my right hand I shall not be disturbed.''

II Corinthians 4:7-''This treasure we possess in earthen vessels to make it clear that its surpassing power comes from God and not from us.''

Psalm 62:7-''He only is my rock and my salvation, my stronghold; I shall not be disturbed.''

35

JOGGING WITH JESUS

Not long ago I was leading a retreat for priests in London, Ontario. One of the priests observed how many joggers were on the road close to the retreat house. He noticed that they came from early morning even before daylight until late at night. They jogged in rain and cold, wind and snow. Nothing deterred them.

This good priest admitted: "If I could be as solicitous about my spiritual health as these joggers are about their physical conditioning, I would be a better person and a holier priest."

His observation struck home. How very true that is for me too. I am sure we have a lot of company in that category, for most of us could say the same about our own prayer life.

We are certainly concerned about staying fit physically, but somehow we do not show that same concern about our spiritual welfare. Speaking for myself, I must confess I rarely miss a meal, but at times there just doesn't seem to be enough time for prayer.

St. Paul manifests his pastoral concern using the image of running:

"You know that while all the runners in the stadium take part in the race, the award goes to one man. In that case, run so as to win! Athletes deny themselves all sorts of things. They do this to win a crown of leaves that withers, but we a crown that is imperishable" (I Cor. 9:24,25).

The Apostle's words go directly to the heart of the matter. There is much food for reflection in his remarks. St. Paul ran his own race well, and he could justifiably say:

"As I look to the Day of Christ, you give me cause to boast that I did not run the race in vain or work to no purpose" (Phil. 2:16).

When Jesus invited us to come follow him, he did not specify if we should walk, run or jog. Certainly jogging would indicate a greater eagerness to follow his footsteps.

Jogging is good exercise, and it serves an important purpose in our lives. God wants us to maintain a rhythm in our lives. This means time for rest, exercise, eating, work and prayer, each in its proper proportion.

In fact we can accomplish two things at once. Many joggers tell me that they pray as they jog. The rhythmic pace of jogging is conducive to reflection.

As we run with Jesus and for Jesus, we are following the example of St. Paul:

"My entire attention is on the finish line as I run toward the prize to which God calls me—life on high in Christ Jesus. All of us who are spiritually mature must have this attitude"(Phil. 3:14,15).

If you are a jogger, perhaps it might be well to read one of the following scriptural passages over and over again until it becomes a part of you, then reflect on it as you jog with Jesus. Sitting quietly with the Lord can be an even more effective method of entering into a deeper, more personal relationship with him.

Micah 6:8-"You have been told, O Man, what is good, and what the Lord requires of you: Only to do the right and to love goodness, and to walk humbly with your God."

Proverbs 2:7,8-"He has counsel in store for the upright, he is the shield of those who walk honestly, guarding the paths of justice, protecting the way of his pious ones."

Ephesians 6:16,17-"In all circumstances hold faith up before you as your shield; . . . Take the helmet of salvation and the sword of the spirit, the Word of God."

Mark 12:30-". . . love the Lord your God with all your heart, with all your soul, with all your mind, and with all your strength."

Ephesians 6:18-"At every opportunity pray in the Spirit, using prayers and petitions of every sort."

Mark 13:33–37-"Be constantly on the watch! Stay awake! You do not know when the appointed time will come. . . . Look around you! You do not know when the master of the house is coming, whether at dusk, at midnight, when the cock crows, or at early dawn. Do not let him come suddenly and catch you asleep. What I say to you, I say to all: Be on guard!"

Matthew 25:20, 21-"The man who had received the five thousand came forward bringing the additional five. 'My lord,' he said, ' you let me have five thousand. See, I have made five thousand more. His master said to him, 'Well done! You are an industrious and reliable servant. Since you were dependable in a small matter I will put you in charge of larger affairs. Come, share your master's joy!' "

36

ROCKING IS LOVING

Not long ago I boarded a plane to fly to a distant city. When I found the seat assigned to me, I discovered that the passenger sitting next to me was a gracious grandmother. She lost no time in beginning what turned out to be a delightful conversation. She told me that she did not like to fly, but it was the quickest way to reach her destination.

She went on to tell me that her daughter had twin boys a few weeks before, and that she was going to help her daughter and also to visit with the rest of her grandchildren. I asked what her chief duty would be. She leaned over to tell me that she was going to spend a lot of time just rocking the twins and her other small grandchildren.

When I suggested that she might spoil her grandchildren, she explained that little ones, even infants, are aware that when they are being 'rocked', they are being loved. With a shrug of her shoulders she said apodictically: "Rocking is loving."

This dear grandmother then went on to give me quite a lesson in caring for small children. She is convinced that very many people suffer from a lack of love in their infancy and childhood, and even in their adult life. She went on to say that in our age mothers and fathers are just too busy to spend much time in 'rocking' their children. I had to agree with her when she said that our modern living is taking its toll in depriving children of much needed love because their parents are so preoccupied. There are so many demands made on parents which prevent them from giving their children all the attention they need.

She had one more precious jewel to share with me. Almost in a whisper, as if meant for my ears only, she said that our modern homes are just not built large enough to house grandparents with the family. That is tragic, she said, because children miss so much rocking and loving. All the time my gracious travelling companion was speaking, she was rocking back and forth in her seat. As the flight attendant passed our seats, she noticed that our dear grandmother was swaying back and forth. She paused to ask if everything was all right. When she was assured that everything was fine, she continued down the aisle.

I pushed my seat back and reflected on the wisdom propounded by this lovely grandmother as she shared her thoughts with me. God created each one of us to love and to be loved. When we are accepted and loved, we can take ourselves just as we are. Our self-image is wholesome. Futhermore, when we know that God loves us, then we are happy and at peace with ourselves.

Since we need to know that we are lovable, our heavenly Father tells us in so many different ways that he loves us. And he loves us just as we are, with all our humanness. We need to hear that often at the very core of our being.

I am not sure of any place in Scripture where God tells us that he will 'rock' us, but he does say that we are precious in his sight and that he does love us. He loves us so much he keeps us in the palm of his hand.

Above all, he loves us so much that he gave us his only Son that we might have life through him. Picture yourself resting in God's arms as he tells you how much he loves you.

Psalm 131:1–3-". . . I have stilled and quieted my soul like a weaned child on its mother's lap. . . . "

Isaiah 43:1–4-". . . Because you are precious in my eyes and glorious, and because I love you, . . . "

Isaiah 49:15-". . . I will never forget you."

John 3:16-"Yes, God so loved the world that he gave his only Son, . . . "

John 15:9-"As the Father has loved me, so I have loved you. . . . "

John 15:13-"There is no greater love than this: to lay down one's life for one's friends."

I John 4:10-"Love, then, consists in this: not that we have loved God, but that he has loved us and has sent his Son as an offering for our sins."

37

A LITTLE RECHARGING

One of the most practical instruments used during the wintry months are jumper cables. How often they have come to the rescue of a stranded driver. How often they have saved a towing job or a long walk home.

Some of us know from first-hand experience how easy it is to forget to turn off the headlights when we park our car. What a frustrating and self-incriminating feeling on our return to the car to discover the battery dead, or at best too weak to turn the motor over fast enough to get it running.

Help! Any Good Samaritan with jumper cables in the vicinity?

Recently as I was returning to my car in the parking lot, a gentleman approached me and apologetically asked if I had any jumper cables. When I assured him I did, he breathed a sigh of relief. It was a simple task to get his car started with a little boost from my own well-charged battery. We both drove off happy.

As I drove homeward, I began to reflect on how easily our spiritual batteries can be drained. When we are too easily angered, impatient, discouraged, disheartened—then we should check our spiritual battery. When we lack motivation or inspiration, it would be well for us to observe our amp gauge or have our battery tested.

Jesus invited us to come to him when our spiritual battery needs recharging. He said plainly: "Apart from me, you can do nothing"(Jn. 15:5). How gracious is his invitation to "Come by yourselves to an out-of-the-way place and rest a little" (Mk. 6:31).

On another occasion his invitation carried with it a promise: "Come to me, all you who are weary and find life burdensome, and I will refresh you"(Mt. 11:28).

Jesus himself showed us the necessity of recharging our spiritual batteries. How often he sought refuge in an olive grove, a desert place or a mountain top to be alone with his father, to be rejuvenated.

In the Good News we read: "Rising early the next morning, he went off to a lonely place in the desert; there he was absorbed in prayer" (Mk. 1:35). At another time Luke says: "Then he went out to the mountain to pray, spending the night in communion with God" (Lk. 6:12). If Jesus' battery needed recharging, how much more so does ours!

Another thought crossed my mind as I drove along. Jesus founded his kingdom as a community based on love. We need one another. We need to help each other.

If our car battery goes dead, we need a charge from a friendly battery. Our own battery cannot recharge itself. If another person is willing to share his battery with us, even momentarily, our car will soon begin to purr like a kitten.

I wonder if St. Paul knew anything about batteries when he advised us: "Help carry one another's

burdens; in that way you will fulfill the law of Christ"
(Gal. 6:2).

Daily meeting the Lord in his Word will help us
recharge our batteries to fulfill our mission in life.

*Philippians 1:9–11-"My prayer is that your love may
more and more abound. . . ."*

*Galatians 6:9-"Let us not grow weary of doing good;
if we do not relax our efforts, in due time we shall
reap our harvest."*

*Isaiah 48:18-"If you would hearken to my com-
mandments, your prosperity would be like a river,
and your vindication like the waves of the sea;"*

*Judith 9:11-". . . 'You are the God of the lowly, the
helper of the oppressed, the supporter of the weak,
the protector of the forsaken, the savior of those
without hope."*

*I Thessalonians 5:14-"We exhort you to admonish
the unruly; cheer the fainthearted; support the
weak; be patient toward all."*

*Psalm 91:2-"Say to the Lord 'My refuge and my for-
tress, my God, in whom I trust.' "*

*I Thessalonians 5:15-"See that no one returns evil to
any other; always seek one another's good and,
for that matter, the good of all."*

38

BIRD-WATCHING AT THE BEACH

All living creatures habitating around the sea speak to us of the creating and providing love of God. Sitting quietly on the beach and listening in the depth of our being to the call of the many species of birds, with the roar of the ocean as background music, is a novel experience. If we close our eyes, our listening and receptivity becomes even keener.

Who of us have not been enthralled by the speed of a spindle-legged sandpiper streaking back and forth with the incoming or receding surf to gather a morsel of food. How instinctively these little creatures can judge the termination of the flow of the surf.

It is intriguing to watch the numerous seagulls hovering over the water. Their enormous wing span makes their movements graceful. They keep their eyes riveted expectantly on the moving water looking for something edible to sustain themselves. Their heads seem to be hanging down as they are on the alert.

When they spy some tempting food, their maneuverability surprises us as they dive upon some unsuspecting prey. If someone should feed them, how quickly they flock together to devour the food. In the process their chatter grows into a raucous crescendo.

The ducks flying in endless procession up and down the beach are another wonder to behold. Apparently, they forage for food in one area and go to another to rest for the night.

As we bird-watch, we hear Jesus underlining the Father's providential love for us by pointing to the birds:

> "Look at the birds in the sky. They do not sow or reap, they gather nothing into barns; yet your heavenly Father feeds them. Are you not more important than they?" (Mt. 6:26).

This is only one tiny phase of God's creation which hovers about the water. The ocean itself teems with such a variety of aquatic life which we cannot see. It hides most of these creatures under its water blanket.

With the psalmist we, too, lift our hearts in praise to the creative genius of our loving Father:

> "How manifold are your works, O Lord!. . . The sea also, great and wide, in which are schools without number of living things both small and great" (Ps. 104:24,25).

We can find God in all the magnificent works of his creation. The might and magnitude of the ocean speaks eloquently to us of his presence and power. We may wish to shout his praises above the roar of the water, or we may wish to sit quietly on the beach and listen to the Lord asking: "What more should I have created which I have not yet created?"

In the solitude of our own heart, let us listen to what he is saying to us in prayer.

Genesis 1:20-". . . Let the water teem with an abundance of living creatures, and on the earth let birds fly beneath the dome of the sky."

Psalm 50:11-"I know all the birds of the air, and whatever stirs in the plains, belongs to me."

Luke 9:58-". . . The foxes have lairs, the birds of the sky have nests, but the Son of Man has nowhere to lay his head."

Psalm 104:16-17-"Well watered are the trees of the Lord. . . . In them the birds build their nests; fir trees are the home of the stork."

Psalm 104:27, 28-"They all look to you to give them food in due time. When you give it to them, they gather it, when you open your hand, they are filled with good things."

Revelation 15:3–4-"Mighty and wonderful are your works, Lord God Almighty!. . . . Your mighty deeds are clearly seen."

Luke 12:6–7-"Are not five sparrows sold for a few pennies? Yet not one of them is neglected by God. In very truth, even the hairs of your head are counted! Fear nothing, then. You are worth more than a flock of sparrows."

39

GOURDS

On my walk through the desert I came upon some wild gourds. The autumn frost had killed the vines, but the green and yellow gourds were lying about in profusion. I picked one up and wiped off the sand. As I held it in my hand, it triggered some personal reflections.

In many ways I am like a gourd. I have such a tough exterior. Like a gourd my exterior becomes a hard shell, which helps me ward off anything which might threaten me. It protects me against my own insecurities and helps me put up a defense when I am criticized, or my opinions challenged, or rejection looms up.

My reflections continued. Inside the gourd is dry and hollow. Like the gourd, I too, am empty and hollow.

Jesus wants to come to me to fill me with his divine life. He wants to dwell with me and within me. Unfortunately I offer so much resistance. I am afraid to be possessed by God. He will ask too much of me if I give him full rein in my life.

Like the gourd my shell is hard to penetrate. It is very brittle. When we attempt to pierce the shell of the gourd, it shatters into many fragments. When Jesus wants to make his home in me, I come apart at the seams like an old wineskin. Jesus gently reminds me, "Unless the grain of wheat falls to the earth and dies, it remains just a grain of wheat. But if it dies, it produces much fruit" (Jn. 12:24).

Jesus wants to penetrate my shell and be a part of my life. How reassuring are his words: "Here I stand, knocking at the door. If anyone hears me calling and opens the door, I will enter his house and have supper with him, and he with me" (Rev. 3:20). I remember, too, that the latch-string is on the inside. I alone can lift the latch.

Again Jesus assures me: "Anyone who loves me will be true to my word, and my Father will love him; we will come to him and make our dwelling place with him" (Jn. 14:23).

Only Jesus can heal my brokenness. Only Jesus can fill my emptiness.

He is a gentleman; He does not force himself upon me. He respects my free will. He waits for me to let him in.

"Come, Lord Jesus!" (Rev. 22:20).

Jesus is present in his Word. Meeting him regularly, even daily as we pray his Word will have a transforming effect upon us.

Philippians 2:13-"It is God who, in his good will toward you, begets in you any measure of desire or achievement."

John 1:11,12-"To his own he came, yet his own did not accept him. Any who did accept him he empowered to become children of God."

Luke 13:34-"O Jerusalem, Jerusalem, you slay the prophets and stone those who are sent to you! How often have I wanted to gather your children together as a mother bird collects her young under her wings, and you refused me!"

Luke 19:41,42-"Coming within sight of the city, he wept over it and said: "If only you had known the path to peace this day; but you have completely lost it from view!. . ."

I Corinthians 6:19-"You must know that your body is a temple of the Holy Spirit, who is within—the Spirit you have received from God. . . ."

II Chronicles 36:13-". . . He became stiffnecked and hardened his heart rather than return to the Lord, . . ."

John 1:14-"The Word became flesh and made his dwelling among us, and we have seen his glory: the glory of an only Son coming from the Father, filled with enduring love."

40

RIVERS OF LIVING WATER

I stood in awe and reverence before the roaring, rushing tons of water cascading down over Niagara Falls. The power and force of this voluminous river was evident as it crashed down over the falls with a deafening roar. The brilliant sun tinted the mist rising above the tumbling water and foam. Little rainbows vied with each other to display the reflected beauty of the sun. From my viewpoint I could begin to appreciate the immensity of this world-wonder.

How often Sacred Scripture symbolizes God's divine life and love as "living water". In a song of thanksgiving, the Prophet Isaiah speaks about God as our loving Savior. He assures us that "with joy you will draw water at the fountain of salvation" (Is. 12:3). The immensity of Niagara Falls baffles our imagination, yet in comparison with the infinite "fountain of salvation", it is merely a microscopic trickle.

Jesus also explained the divine indwelling with us and within us as "living water". This divine life forms our union with him. Our union with Jesus, dwelling within us, is our foretaste of heaven. In this life we can only be partially filled with his divine life and love. Our capacity to receive his divine life is like a thimble trying to catch all the water pouring over Niagara Falls. When we shed this mortal coil in death, then we will have a much greater capacity to receive his living water. It is this divine life, this 'living water', which will bring us eternal life.

Jesus explained this great mystery in these few words: "Whoever drinks the water I give him will never be thirsty; no, the water I give shall become a fountain within him, leaping up to provide eternal life" (Jn. 4:14).

Jesus invites us to come to him to receive this influx of his divine life and love. He then asks us to become his emissaries by radiating his presence and sharing his divine life with those whom he sends across our path each day. He gives us the assurance that he will use us as channels of his "living water" to others if we but let him.

Listen to his own words: "If anyone thirsts, let him come to me; let him drink who believes in me . . . From within him rivers of living water shall flow" (Jn. 7:37,38). How easy our apostolate becomes! Jesus asks us to permit him to fill us first; and then he wants to use us as a channel through which he can touch others.

Incidentally, this gives us our true dignity as Christians. We are Christians not because we worship in a certain way, or because we believe a set of doctrines, or follow a specific moral code. No, we are Christians because Christ is dwelling within us, because we have been receptive to his indwelling within us. Because we have accepted his indwelling in faith, therefore we pray, believe and live according to his Way.

By this time the spray from the Falls had dampened my clothing considerably. However, my spirits were not in the least dampened. On the contrary, my heart was singing with joy as I witnessed the might and power of God, especially at the immense out-pouring of his love. May the Word of God keep our hearts ever joyous, ever grateful.

Isaiah 55:1-"All you who are thirsty, come to the water!"

Revelation 22:1-"The angel then showed me the river of life-giving water, clear as a crystal, which issued from the throne of God and of the Lamb. . . ."

John 3:5-"I solemnly assure you, no one can enter into God's kingdom without being begotten of water and Spirit."

Matthew 10:42-"Whoever gives a cup of cold water to one of these lowly ones because he is a disciple will not want for his reward."

Revelation 7:17-". . . the Lamb on the throne will shepherd them. He will lead them to springs of life-giving water. . . ."

John 13:5-"Then he poured water into a basin and began to wash his disciples' feet and dry them with the towel he had around him."

Psalm 105:41-"He cleft the rock, and the water gushed forth; it flowed through the dry lands like a stream."

41

THE SMILE OF GOD

When I returned to my room, I discovered that someone had lovingly placed two exquisite rosebuds in a little vase on my desk. I was deeply touched and pleased at this act of kindness, as roses are special to me. How aptly someone has said: "A rose is the smile of God." Surely every rose is a silent witness to God's creative genius. The rose is also the symbol of love and St. John says: "God is love" (I Jn. 4:16).

As I admired these beautiful buds, my thoughts carried me back to the rose plant itself. The stock is a complete chemical laboratory, responsible for the whole process of growth and development of every part of the plant. The roots absorb nourishment from the soil, the leaves drink in the sunshine and fresh air, the stock supports and diffuses the life-giving elements in proper proportion to every segment of the plant.

As I sat in awe and wonder, I asked myself who planned the delicate tint of each petal, especially the golden thread woven so intricately at the edge of each petal. No one other than God, himself.

How simple was his command: "Let the earth bring forth vegetation: every kind of plant that bears seed and every kind of fruit tree on earth that bears fruit with its seed in it . . . . God looked at everything he had made and he found it very good" (Gen. 1:11, 31). Yes, God's word is simple, but how mysterious the process and how magnificent the product!

If we listen carefully with our heart, we can hear God saying to us: "What more could I have created for you that I have not already done?"

Jesus reminds us of the creative love of the Father when he says: "Learn a lesson from the way the wild flowers grow. They do not work; they do not spin. Yet I assure you, not even Solomon in all his splendor was arrayed like one of these" (Mt. 6:28,29).

Unlike the poet who sang of a certain flower wasting its sweetness on the desert air, the roses on my desk were perfuming the whole room. That is precisely what God is asking of us.

St. Paul emphasizes our role in these words: "Thanks be to God who unfailingly leads us on in Christ's triumphal train, and employs us to diffuse the fragrance of his knowledge everywhere! We are an aroma of Christ for God's sake, both among those who are being saved and those on the way to destruction" (II Cor. 2:14,15).

Sirach encourages us to praise God our Creator, using this beautiful metaphor:

"Listen my faithful children: open up your petals, like roses planted near running waters; send up the sweet odor of incense, break forth in blossoms like the lily. Send up the sweet odor of your hymn of praise; bless the Lord for all he has done" (Sir. 39:13,14).

Let us be a rose spreading the fragrance of God's love everywhere. As we bask in his presence listening to his Word, he will nurture us as he does the rose.

Psalm 9:11-"They trust in you who cherish your name, for you forsake not those who see you, O Lord."

Mark 9:23, 24-". . . 'Everything is possible to a man who trusts.' The boy's father immediately exclaimed, 'I do believe! Help my lack of trust!' "

Nahum 1:7-"The Lord is good, a refuge on the day of distress; he takes care of those who have recourse to him."

Deuteronomy 32:10-". . . He shielded them and cared for them, guarding them as the apple of his eye."

Ephesians 5:29-"Observe that no one ever hates his own flesh; no, he nourishes it and takes care of it as Christ cares for the Church-"

I Peter 5:7-"Cast all your cares on him because he cares for you."

Sirach 40:27-"The fear of God is a paradise of blessings; its canopy, all that is glorious."

42

A TINY GLOW

My friend, John, has a very deep and personal relationship with God the Father. He graciously shared with me the origin of that friendship.

John was born in Ireland and spent his entire youth on the Emerald Isle on a small farm. He had to take a bus to and from school. However, the bus stopped one and a half miles from his home. He had to walk the rest of the way. John dreaded the wintertime since it was already dark when the bus arrived at his stop. He was frightened by the darkness and dreaded the long walk home.

Frequently, as he alighted from the bus, John could see a tiny red glow in the dark at the bus stop. He knew it was the glow of his father's cigarette as he had come to accompany his son home.

His father always greeted him warmly and listened to all the happenings of the day at school while they walked down the road to their home. For John it was the most cherished time of the day since his father's protective presence removed any shadow of fear from him. Even more, it gave both of them an opportunity to enjoy each other's company. John can still recall many of the things which his father shared with him as together they walked down that country lane.

John assured me that this was the beginning of his

appreciation of the Fatherhood of God. For him it was a powerful reflection of our heavenly Father's caring and concerned love watching over us at every moment of the day.

How encouragingly our heavenly Father assures us that he is our loving Abba. He tells us that he has definite plans for us:

"I know well the plans I have in mind for you . . . plans for your welfare, not for woe! plans to give you a future full of hope."

He is attentive to all our prayers: "When you call me, when you go to pray to me, I will listen to you."

He assures us that he is always with us and never abandons us:

"When you look for me, you will find me. Yes, when you seek me with all your heart, you will find me with you" (Jer. 29:11-14).

Even a brief reflection on these words of our Father will enrich and deepen our relationship with him. If we continue our reflection using one of the following scriptural passages as a starting point, our love and friendship with our Abba will be greatly deepened and enriched.

John 14:23-". . . my Father will love him; we will come to him and make our dwelling place with him."

John 16:27-"The Father already loves you, because

129

you have loved me and have believed that I came from God."

John 14:6-". . . No one comes to the Father but through me."

John 6:37-"All that the Father gives me shall come to me; no one who comes will I ever reject,"

John 6:32–33-". . . It is my Father who gives you the real heavenly bread. God's bread comes down from heaven and gives life to the world."

John 6:44-"No one can come to me unless the Father who sent me draws him; I will raise him up on the last day."

John 17:21-"That all may be one as you, Father, are in me, and I in you; I pray that they may be one in us, that the world may believe that you sent me."

43

THAT EXTRA STEP

On a recent trip I took a flight which made several intermediate stops at a number of small towns. At each stop the pilot of the airplane came back into the cabin to visit with the passengers. He was very friendly and outgoing.

When he visited with me, he told me that his wife and three of his children were killed some five years ago by a drunken driver. Just a month before I met him, his only surviving son, age 24, was also a traffic fatality. Once again this accident was caused by an intoxicated driver.

In spite of the tragedy in his life, this man seemed to have a certain peace about him. His attitude did not reveal any self pity; there was no bitterness toward God, nor toward the persons responsible for these tragedies. He confirmed my observation when he said: "I am at peace, and I pray for all those who were involved in these deaths."

When we arrived at our destination, the pilot walked up the jetway with me. As we came into the terminal, he saw an elderly woman looking anxiously toward the plane from which we had just disembarked.

Characteristically, the pilot immediately went over to her and asked if she were expecting someone. When she informed him that she was to meet her elderly sister, he asked her on which flight she was to arrive. When he discovered that it was another flight arriving at a different gate, he put down his bags, took her arm and accompanied her down the concourse to the right gate.

I greatly admired this man who had not only piloted our plane safely to our destination, but who had managed to guide his own life into the way of peace. How many people he must have touched with his gentle, loving concern.

Of a certainty this man was trying to live the Gospel way of life. We, too, have the obligation to make the Good News known by our very lifestyle. We can do so in many different ways. As we permit the Holy Spirit to mold and transform us so that we have the attitudes and mentality of Jesus within us, then we will reflect and radiate the way of life which Jesus set forth. Our life will be characterized by loving concern for others and a great peace and joy within our hearts.

This transformation takes place within us when we realize that God loves us with a caring, concerned, forgiving, enduring love. He loves us just as we are.

As we meet Jesus in his Word each day, he will transform this mentality and attitude into a habit pattern which will automatically govern our lives in every given situation. May these suggested Scriptures have that transforming power.

I Corinthians 9:16-". . . I am under compulsion and have no choice. I am ruined if I do not preach it!"

Philippians 4:19,20-"My God in turn will supply your needs fully, in a way worthy of his magnificent riches in Christ Jesus. All glory to our God and Father for unending ages! Amen."

Mark 4:24-". . . Listen carefully to what you hear. In the measure you give you shall receive, and more besides."

Galatians 5:13-". . . Out of love, place yourselves at one another's service."

Luke 6:38-"Give and it shall be given to you. Good measure, pressed down, shaken together, running over, will they pour into the fold of your garment. For the measure you measure with will be measured back to you."

Romans 12:10,11-"Love one another with the affection of brothers. Anticipate each other in showing respect. Do not grow slack but be fervent in spirit; he whom you serve is the Lord."

Philippians 4:10-"It gave me great joy in the Lord that your concern for me bore fruit once more. You had been concerned all along, of course, but lacked the opportunity to show it."

44

WHERE THE DEER AND THE ANTELOPE ROAM

As I was journeying across the prairie, I stopped to rest and also to enjoy the beauty of God's creation. As I pulled the car off the highway, I spotted four antelopes close to the roadway.

As I got out of the car slowly, they watched me with suspicious eyes, prepared to bolt away if I threatened them in any way. When they discovered that I meant them no harm, they began to relax. They no longer stared to watch my every movement, but they began looking about in other directions. In fact, one of them began to graze once again, totally disregarding my presence.

These fleet-footed and sleek animals were a reminder of the beauty of God's creation. He created them with instincts which would help them to protect and provide for themselves.

However, what impressed me most at the moment was how much these antelopes trusted me. After they observed me for a while, they seemed to sense that I intended them no harm. Immediately, they began to calm down and relax in my presence. In brief, they trusted me.

The thought occurred to me: how much do I trust? How much do I trust God? Do I unwaveringly give myself to his plans for me?

As Jesus tried to make known the great love that his Father has for us, and as he revealed his own infinite love for us, he asked us to trust him. How often he asked for trust!

On one occasion he said: "Fear is useless. What is needed is trust" (Mk. 5:36).

Another time he said: "Trust me when I tell you that whoever does not accept the kingdom of God as a child will not enter into it"(Lk. 18:17). A little child really trusts those people who love him. He confidently places himself totally in their hands.

The secret of trust is love. When we love a person, we trust that person.

Jesus assures us that "anyone who loves me will be true to my word, and my Father will love him; we will come to him and make our dwelling place with him" (Jn. 14:23). This is how much he loves us.

These beautiful antelopes with their heads and ears pricked up triggered my thoughts about trust as they grazed unafraid even though they knew I was watching them.

As I got back into the car, they watched my every movement without scampering away. As I drove away their eyes were riveted on me. When I looked into the rear view mirror, I could see one of them stretching his neck in order to watch me drive away.

I almost felt like I was leaving a friend, so grateful was I for the trust they showed me and taught me.

Thank you, Lord, for this unusual encounter on my journey back to you. Increase my love so that I may trust you implicitly.

Nehemiah 9:19-"*In your great mercy you did not forsake them in the desert. The column of cloud did not cease to lead them by day on their journey, nor did the column of fire by night cease to light for them the way by which they were to travel.*"

Psalm 42:2,3-"*As the hind longs for the running waters, so my soul longs for you, O God. Athirst is my soul for God, the living God.*"

Habakkuk 3:19-"*God, my Lord, is my strength; he makes my feet swift as those of hinds and enables me to go upon the heights.*"

John 14:1—"Do not let your hearts be troubled. Have faith in God and faith in me."

Psalm 28:7—"The Lord is my strength and my shield. In him my heart trusts, and I find help; then my heart exults, and with my song I give him thanks."

I Corinthians 13:7-"There is no limit to love's forbearance, to its trust, its hope, its power to endure."

45

PRICKLY PROTECTION

It was late in the fall of the year. The first killing frost had foraged forth to snuff out all the beautiful flowers of the summer. The wilted, drooping flowers were harbingers of the wintry blasts which would soon follow.

As I sat at the window enjoying a cup of coffee, I noticed in the flower bed below the window one sole survivor of the devastating frost. It was a yellow snapdragon which had grown up in the protective custody of a thorny barberry shrub. This daring flower had grown right up through the center of the barberry bush with its flowery bloom projecting itself above the shrub.

Through the growing season this barberry plant had enfolded the snapdragon in its prickly arms. Its spiny branches had shielded the snapdragon from any and all would-be marauders in search of flowers. At this season of the year, the barberry was trying to blanket this annual flower against the chill of this early frost.

This delicate snapdragon was unlike the seed which Jesus described in the Gospel that fell among thorns only to be choked by those thorns when it sprouted up. On the contrary, this plant thrived because of the protecting fortress which the barberry formed around it.

As I lingered over my coffee, I noticed, too, what a beautiful color combination these two plants produced. The profusion of tiny russet-colored leaves on the barberry plant formed a contrasting background for the rich yellow of the snapdragon. This in turn was dotted with the deep red berries of the barberry. The Master-Painter had done his work well. Thank you, Lord!

As I enjoyed this unusual picture, I thought of how much our lives resemble this setting before me. We encounter many thorns and barbs along our pathway through life. From time to time they can cause us pain and suffering. Sometimes their thorns pierce deeply. At other times they scratch our skin with a painful burning sensation. We cannot always understand the reason for their existence. We try to avoid them as much as possible.

However, viewed from the perspective of time, we often see how these traumatic and tragic experiences in life were real blessings in disguise.

Like the barberry bush these thorns in life might protect us from more pernicious onslaughts. They condition and prepare us for other more painful fortunes in life.

Even though the thorns might have seemed a bit sharp at times, they were the crosses which Jesus invited us to take up daily in order to be his followers.

Our prayer like the prayer of Jesus may well be: "Father, if it is your will, take this cup from me." Like Jesus we must always be willing to conform to what the Father deems best for us; hence we, too, add: "yet not my will but yours be done" *(Lk. 22:42)*

As we pray with his Word, we will not only see God's will more clearly, but we will be encouraged and strengthened to fulfill it in our lives. The following passages will prove helpful.

Isaiah 41:10-"Fear not, I am with you; be not dismayed; I am your God. I will strengthen you, and help you, and uphold you with my right hand of justice."

Wisdom 3:5-"Chastised a little, they shall be greatly blessed, because God tried them and found them worthy of himself."

Sirach 2:4,5-". . . Accept whatever befalls you, in crushing misfortune be patient; for in fire gold is tested, and worthy men in the crucible of humiliation."

Ephesians 5:17–20-"Do not continue in ignorance, but try to discern the will of the Lord. . . . Give thanks to God the Father always and for everything in the Name of our Lord Jesus Christ."

Galatians 5:24-"Those who belong to Christ Jesus have crucified their flesh with its passions and desires."

Matthew 6:27–29-"Which of you by worrying can add a moment to his life-span? As for clothes, why be concerned? Learn a lesson from the way the wild flowers grow. They do not work; they do not spin. Yet I assure you, not even Solomon in all his splendor was arrayed like one of these."

Psalm 61:2–4-"Hear, O God, my cry; listen to my prayer! From the earth's end I call to you as my heart grows faint. You will set me high upon a rock; you will give me rest, for you are my refuge, a tower of strength against the enemy."

46

STAY IN TOUCH

I received notice that a person, who was very dear to me at one time, was called home to God. It was a sudden and unexpected death.

Naturally I began to reminisce about our friendship. We were once close neighbors. We had so many things in common. We often visited over a cup of coffee, and shared much of our lives. How often we supported and encouraged one another. We really enjoyed just being together.

Then it all happened. My friend moved to a city nearly 1500 miles away. At first we corresponded faithfully. We called long distance on special occasions or if something unexpected occurred.

At first my friend wanted to be kept updated on all the happenings in the neighborhood. I tried to do that each time I wrote. For my part I was very much interested in all the new things which were happening in my friend's new environment.

Gradually our letters became fewer and came at irregular intervals. We did not call anymore. The only word I sent this past year was a Christmas card with just a little note.

As I mused about our friendship which had waned so much, I asked myself: Why did this take place? The answer was very clear. Our interests were different since we lived in different areas of the country and both of us made new friends.

As I pondered this situation, I got a clearer insight into what St. Paul said so many times. He made a lot of sense. St. Paul insists that we pray always. He repeats it over and over again using such expressions as "Pray perseveringly," "Pray constantly and attentively," and "never cease praying."

St. Paul's counsel is wise. If I want Jesus to be a good friend of mine, and if I want to be His friend, then I must stay in touch with Him. If I want to enrich and deepen my relationship with Jesus, I must meet him regularly, even daily, in prayer; otherwise our friendship will soon wane.

Friendship is built on mutual interest. If I do not spend time with the Lord, then my interests will turn to other things, and I will soon become oblivious of his loving presence and his providential care and concern for me.

How correct is St. Paul's admonition: "Be intent on things above rather than on things of earth" *(Col. 3:2)*. St. Augustine says that we pray without ceasing by desiring to reach our home in heaven.

The most fruitful way of staying in touch with Jesus is to listen to his Word. Did he not say that those who hear his word and keep it would be blessed?

Luke 18:9–14-"O God, be merciful to me, a sinner. . . ."

Luke 11:1–4-"Lord, teach us to pray. . . ."

Colossians 4:2-"Pray perseveringly, be attentive to prayer, and pray in a spirit of thanksgiving."

I Peter 4:7-11-"Do not be perturbed; remain calm so that you will be able to pray."

I Thessalonians 5:16–18-"Rejoice always, never cease praying, render constant thanks; such is God's will for you in Christ Jesus."

Ephesians 6:18-"Pray constantly and attentively for all in the holy company."

Matthew 26:41-"Be on guard, and pray that you may not undergo the test."

47

OUR HANDS SPEAK

Someone has said: "If God seems far away, who do you think moved?" How far away is God from us?

God is no farther away than our hands. Our hands continually reveal the creative genius of our loving Father. Pause momentarily to reflect on our hands. How dexterous God has made them.

With the agility and strength of our hands we can pick up a tiny pin or move a large rock. Trained and gifted hands can render a piano concert or type a flawless letter.

Our hands speak eloquently. With our hands we communicate our feelings, our attitudes, our love and even, God forbid, our rejection of someone.

A handshake is quite revealing. It may at times tell a friend how delighted we are to see him or her. It may at times tell another person that we are indifferent to his presence. The same hands can reveal feelings of warmth and love or coldness and unfriendliness.

A helping hand reveals our loving concern for others. An embrace, a little pat or holding another person's hand expresses our love for that person.

Holding the hand of a person who is ill or suffering great pain will bring comfort and consolation to that person.

With gestures our hands help us to make our words more emphatic and lucid. They aid us in expressing our thoughts and feelings.

Our hands can also wound, causing deep inner pain by a gesture of ridicule or rejection. Countless are the ways we can inflict physical pain with our hands.

Hands can also express an inner attitude of prayerful union with God. We have all enjoyed the beautiful picture entitled 'Praying Hands'—an inspiring work of art.

Hands devoutly folded in prayer reveal a heart filled with love and reverence, a heart humbly recognizing our poverty of spirit before the Lord.

Hands lifted up with palms raised heavenward are a gesture of oblation, an offering of ourselves to our gracious Father. This same gesture tells our Abba that we are open and ready to receive whatever he wishes to send us.

Hands lifted up are an expression of praise and thanksgiving to a Father whose creative love gifted us with hands.

"Hands held aloft" is an eloquent prayer of petition to our provident Father. St. Paul writes: "It is my wish, then, that in every place the men shall offer prayers with blameless hands held aloft, and be free from anger and dissension" (I Tim. 2:8). When our hands are raised in prayer, a great healing takes place. It is hard to be angry when our hands are raised heavenward.

Thank you, Lord, for the gift of my hands!

Psalm 88:10-"Daily I call upon you, O Lord; to you I stretch out my hands."

I Thessalonians 4:11-"Work with your hands as we directed you to do. . . . "

Ephesians 4:28-"Let him work with his hands at honest labor so that he will have something to share with those in need."

Psalm 28:2-"Hear the sound of my pleading, when I cry to you, lifting up my hands toward your holy shrine."

Psalm 47:2-"All you peoples, clap your hands, shout to God with cries of gladness. . . . "

Mark 10:13–16-"Then he embraced them and blessed them, placing his hands on them."

Proverbs 31:20-"She reaches out her hands to the poor, and extends her arms to the needy."

48

HOOT HOOT

A whole colony of owls have made their home in my neighborhood. Every night they chant their mournful chorus to the moon and stars.

I like to walk out-of-doors at night to visit with these strange birds. They perch themselves on the very top of the highest trees at some distance from each other. Then, they maintain a chorus of hooting back and forth to each other.

When I approach the tree on which one of the owls is perched, it seems to object to my invading its domain as it seems to be hooting at me. I sometimes try to respond to its hooting.

From these high perches I am sure that they are surveying the area in search of food. The owl is a nocturnal bird of prey. Its keen eyesight, its hooked bill and strong talons equip it adequately to be carnivorous.

The ancient Israelites were forbidden to eat the meat of owls. The owl was classified with the unclean food and therefore prohibited. However, it is interesting to note that the law enumerated several species of owls: the screech owl, the barn owl, the desert owl, the little owl and just plain owls. The Hebrews used different words for each species. They made their distinction this precise so that no one would be tempted to break the law by eating any variety of owl for food.

The weird communication of owls in the dark of night reminds me of the sinister 'voices' of evil lurking in the darkness. These 'voices' enamor us and would lead us away from the "Light of the world."

In scriptural language darkness means the presence of evil, wickedness, sin, while light symbolizes the presence of God. Jesus came into the world as its light to conquer evil. "The light shines on in darkness, a darkness that did not overcome it" (Jn. 1:5).

Furthermore, he promised us that if we follow him, we would never be overcome by evil.

"I am the light of the world. No follower of mine shall ever walk in darkness; no, he shall possess the light of life" (Jn. 8:12).

During this brief reflection, I became aware once again of the owls chanting from the treetops their chorus of praise to their Creator.

Even though the owl was considered unclean to the ancient Israelites, and perhaps the owl may not be our favorite bird, we must remember that "God looked at everything he had made, and he found it very good" (Gen. 1:31).

May the Word of God draw us continually into the Light so that we may never walk in Darkness.

Isaiah 65:17–18-"Lo, I am about to create new heavens and a new earth; the things of the past shall not be remembered or come to mind. Instead, there shall always be rejoicing and happiness in what I create; for I create Jerusalem to be a joy and its people to be a delight."

Romans 13:12-". . . Let us cast off the deeds of darkness and put on the armour of light."

II Corinthians 4:6-"For God, who said, 'Let light shine out of darkness,' has shone in our hearts, that we in turn might make known the glory of God shining on the face of Christ."

Ephesians 4:17,18-"I declare and solemnly attest in the Lord that you must no longer live as the pagans do—their minds empty, their understanding darkened. . . . "

Colossians 1:13,14-"He rescued us from the power of darkness and brought us into the kingdom of his beloved Son. Through him we have redemption, the forgiveness of our sins."

John 3:16-"Yes, God so loved the world that he gave his only Son, that whoever believes in him may not die but may have eternal life."

John 17:15,16-"I do not ask you to take them out of the world, but to guard them from the evil one. They are not of the world, any more than I belong to the world."

49

HAPPY BIRTHDAY

I was invited to the home of one of my friends for dinner and an evening with the family. The occasion was the 16th birthday of the eldest son. It was one of the most unusual birthday dinners I ever attended.

The 16-year-old, Bill, was seated at the head of the table. The progress of the dinner went along nicely, with Bill doing the serving. As a teen-ager he did a masterful job of serving the good home-cooked food. During the meal the father and mother, as well as his brothers and sisters, six in all, were directing most of their conversation to Bill.

After the entree and before the dessert—birthday cake and ice cream—was served, a special family ritual began. Each member of the family, including the father and mother, individually expressed to Bill their appreciation of some special deed he had performed or some event in which he participated during the past year, which meant a great deal to that member of the family.

I was amazed at the ease and love with which each member related the happening, and how much they appreciated Bill for it. One said how much she appreciated Bill taking her roller-skating when she could find no one else to go with her. A brother was grateful for the time that Bill mowed the lawn for him. Another sister recalled how Bill got a clutch hit in a crucial baseball game during the summer when he was playing in a local league. She was proud of him. Each member of the family, in turn, thanked Bill or congratulated him for some act of kindness or some feat which he accomplished.

All was not yet over, nor were we ready for the birthday cake now. Next Bill began to address himself to each member of the family individually, expressing his appreciation and admiration for what each member had done for him. His brother had run an errand for him when Bill's bicycle had a flat tire; another loaned him some money when he was short; a sister vacuumed his room for him, and so the litany of thoughtfulness and kindness to one another continued.

Next the presents were brought forth. These, too, were unusual. The presents were not gaily gift-wrapped purchased gifts. No, these gifts were objects which each member of the family had made for Bill, each according to his or her own talent and ability. As Bill opened each present, he thanked the donor with a loving, unembarrassed embrace.

I was so surprised and delighted at this family ritual of celebrating birthdays that I was almost speechless. I just wanted to absorb every nuance of what I was seeing and hearing.

With celebrations such as this one, why should we mind birthdays coming in such quick succession!

Listening to the message which the Lord conveys to us through his Word will deepen our relationship with all those persons God sends into our lives.

Luke 2:51-"He went down with them then, and came to Nazareth, and was obedient to them."

Psalm 133:1–3 "Behold, how good it is, and how pleasant, where brethren dwell as one!...For there the Lord has pronounced his blessing, life forever."

Colossians 3:13- "Bear with one another; forgive whatever grievances you have against one another."

Galatians 5:13- "Out of love, place yourselves at one another's service."

Ephesians 5:21- "Defer to one another out of reverence for Christ."

Matthew 5:23–24- "...Go first to be reconciled with your brother and then come and offer your gift."

I Corinthians 13:4–7- "...There is no limit to love's forbearance, to its trust, its hope, its power to endure."

50

BIRDBATH

Our dining room window looks out upon a three-level birdbath. A little trickle of water gently, and almost imperceptibly, bubbles up in the highest pan which in turn overflows slowly into the lower pan and on to the third and lowest level.

The birds love this bath and frequent it daily. They have become so domesticated that they are not frightened away by anyone watching them, nor are they embarrassed about bathing in public.

I am amazed at the number and variety of birds which seem to come about the same time each day. There are red-breasted robins aplenty, a good number of yellow canaries, finches and sparrows of every hue. It is interesting to observe how many birds can get into a 24-inch pan at the same time. It is even more amusing to watch them splashing and dousing one another in the process. Even those who come only to quench their thirst get their share of water splashed on them.

Never once have I seen one bird pecking, attacking or chasing another one out of the water. Their chirping communication is understandable to God alone, and I am sure that he accepts it as a medley of praise.

As I enjoy this daily ritual, I wonder if St. Paul contemplated such a scene when he advised us to live in harmony with one another. Recall his admonition: "I plead with you . . . to live a life worthy of the calling you have received, with perfect humility, meekness, and patience, bearing with one another lovingly. Make every effort to preserve the unity which has the Spirit as its origin and peace as its binding force" *(Eph. 4:1-3)*.

The Apostle whom Jesus loved speaks often and forcefully about loving one another. How pointedly he writes: "One who has no love for the brother he has seen cannot love the God he has not seen. The commandment we have from him is this: whoever loves God must also love his brother" (I Jn. 4:20, 21).

As two more beautiful canaries alighted for their bath, the words of Jesus came to mind: "Look at the birds in the sky. They do not sow or reap, they gather nothing into barns; yet your heavenly Father feeds them" (Mt. 6:26).

In my quiet reverie I could visualize our heavenly Father looking upon this scene, beholding the birds enjoying themselves and smiling down upon them with his loving concern. He must enjoy it, for the sacred writer tells us: "God looked at everything he had made, and he found it very good" (Gen. 1:31).

How much more joy do we bring to our loving Father when we live in peace and harmony as do these birds. His joy is even greater because Jesus asks: "Are not you more important than they?" (Mt. 6:26).

In his Word, the Lord gives us many directives and much encouragement to accept and love one another.

Matthew 22:39-"You shall love your neighbor as yourself."

Matthew 25:40-"I assure you, as often as you did it for one of my least brothers, you did it for me."

John 13:34-"Love one another. Such as my love has been for you, so must your love be for each other."

Matthew 6:14-"If you forgive the faults of others, your heavenly Father will forgive you yours."

Colossians 3:13-"Bear with one another; forgive whatever grievances you have against one another...."

I John 4:7-"Let us love one another because love is of God...."

Daniel 3:80-"All you birds of the air, bless the Lord; praise and exalt him above all forever."

51

SUNSET

The little world I call home is a land of sunsets. With an expansive view of the western horizon, I can glory in gorgeous sunsets throughout the whole year.

Who of us has not stood entranced in awe and reverence as we behold a celestial sunset? Our loving Father seems to outdo himself as he reflects just an infinitesimal bit of his beauty in each different sunset.

In my imaginative heart I can almost see the Father smiling to himself as he watches his children enjoying the exquisite beauty of his sunsets. He does so much to make us happy and also to remind us of his abiding presence.

Sunset time is usually a time for deceleration after a duty-filled day in our world of speed and confusion. As a rule, most of the preoccupations of the day are behind us, and as evening approaches we are beginning to relax. This gives us more time to drink in the beauty of the sunset. This relaxation also makes us more receptive to enjoying God's handiwork.

The same is true as we grow older in life. As we advance in age, may we, like Jesus, progress steadily "in wisdom and age and grace before God and men" *(Lk. 2:52)*. With most of our years behind us, we can begin to slow down to enjoy more fully and with more leisure the sunset of life. I am sure that Jesus meant all of us, but in a special way all those who have rest in the evening of life, when he invites us to: "Come by yourselves to an out-of-the-way place and rest a little" *(Mk. 6:31)*. A well-rested body is paramount to entering into the prayer of listening.

Certainly it is our privilege as we approach the evening of life, to reminisce. The joy of living helps us see so much beauty that perhaps we have missed in the bustle of our more active days. Furthermore, remembering the generosity of our loving Father, the love of family and friends enhances the joys and happiness of the sunset time of life.

The evening of life deepens our relationship with our Father in heaven. Our more leisurely lifestyle affords us the time to heed his words: "Be still and know that I am God" *(Psalm 46:11)*. Or again: "Wait in patience and know that I am God" *(Psalm 37:7)*.

154

As we linger longer in the sunshine of His presence, we begin to appreciate more and more the kindness of friends and neighbors; we grow in greater affection for our children, and we come to realize what jewels we have in our grandchildren.

All this because the evening of life brings us to the realization that all things and all people are precious gifts in our life coming from an all-good God.

May each day's sunset be a delightful experience for you!

Psalm 116:12-"How shall I make a return to the Lord for all the good he has done for me?"

Hebrews 13:14–16-"For here we have no lasting city; we are seeking one which is to come. . . . Do not neglect good deeds and generosity; God is pleased by sacrifices of that kind."

Psalm 139:5-"Behind me and before, you hem me in and rest your hand upon me."

Psalm 104:1,2-"Bless the Lord, O my soul! O Lord, my God, you are great indeed! You are clothed with majesty and glory, robed in light as with a cloak. . . ."

Psalm 92:15-"They shall bear fruit even in old age; vigorous and sturdy shall they be."

Luke 4:40-"At sunset, all who had people sick with a variety of diseases took them to him, and he laid hands on each of them and cured them."

Psalm 103:1–3-"Bless the Lord, O my soul; and all

*my being, bless his holy name. Bless the Lord, O
my soul, and forget not all his benefits; He par-
dons all your iniquities, he heals all your ills.''*

52

WHAT IS HEAVEN LIKE

When I was a child I worried about heaven. I
could not sing well, and never learned to play a
musical instrument, much less a harp. In my childish
imagination I pictured heaven as a mighty choir of
angels and saints surrounding the throne of God
singing his praises accompanied by the heavenly
music of the harp.

With this impression, I thought that heaven could
become rather dull and boring. One day when my
dear mother was trying to explain to me the true happiness of heaven, I remember asking her: if I was
good and if I went to heaven, did she think that Jesus
would let me go out some day to play with the little devils who must be lingering around the pearly
gates, since they were denied admission. Needless
to say, I was duly reprimanded for my naivete.

Later on in life, I discovered that the great Apostle of the Gentiles had a similar difficulty in trying to

describe heaven. All he could say was: "Eye has not seen, ear has not heard, nor has it so much as dawned on man what God has prepared for those who love him"*(I Cor. 2:9).*

These words of St. Paul simply speak to us of mystery without satisfying our curiousity or our insatiable hunger to know what heaven is like.

Jesus did not tell us what heaven is like for the simple reason that our finite minds could not grasp the other-worldliness of heaven. While Jesus did not tell us what we could expect in heaven, he did teach us the way to reach our eternal destiny.

Jesus gave us the key to understand more fully what heaven is like:

> "Anyone who loves me will be true to my word, and my Father will love him; we will come to him and make our dwelling place with him" *(Jn. 14:23).*

Heaven, then, is our dwelling with God and his dwelling with us. Our heaven began at the moment of our baptism. We were baptized into the Trinitarian life. The Father, Son and Holy Spirit came to live with us and within us. We belong to the family of God, a community of perfect love. As a sponge, we are immersed in his infinte love.

Here on earth, our land of sojourn, each time we die to self and surrender to God in love, we come one step closer to our home in heaven, to our total union with our loving Father.

When we really love a person, we want to be close to that person, to give of ourselves, to enjoy that person's friendship and companionship, to share in his or her joys and sorrows, to be a mutual source of comfort and consolation, to find reciprocal hope and encouragement. Our heavenly Father loves us so much he has come to live with us, to share his divine life with us in this land of exile. Our heaven has already begun.

Experiencing Jesus in prayer is a slight foretaste of the joys of heaven.

John 17:21-"*That all may be one as you, Father, are in me, and I in you. . . .*"

I Corinthians 2:9-"*Eye has not seen, ear has not heard, nor has it so much as dawned on man what God has prepared for those who love him.*"

Colossians 3:1-"*Set your heart on what pertains to higher realms where Christ is seated at God's right hand. . . .*"

II Corinthians 12:3,4-". . . *to hear words which cannot be uttered, words which no man may speak. . . .*"

I Corinthians 15:53-"*this corruptible body must be clothed with incorruptibility, this mortal body with immortality.*"

Revelation 21:3,4-". . . *there shall be no more death or mourning, crying out or pain, for the former world has passed away.*"

John 5:24-". . . *the man who hears my word has faith in him who sent me possesses eternal life.*"

Additional books from
LIVING FLAME PRESS
Available at your bookstore or from
Living Flame Press, Locust Valley, N.Y. 11560

LIVING HERE AND HEREAFTER
Christian Dying,
Death and Resurrection   2.95

Msgr. David E. Rosage. The author offers great comfort
to us by dispelling our fears and anxieties about our life
after this earthly sojourn. Based on God's Word as presented in Sacred Scripture, these brief daily medita-
tions help us understand more clearly and deeply the
meaning of suffering and death.

PRAYING WITH SCRIPTURE
IN THE HOLY LAND
Daily Meditations With the Risen Jesus   3.50

Msgr. David E. Rosage. Herein is offered a daily meeting
with the Risen Jesus in those Holy Places which He
sanctified by His human presence. Three hundred and
sixty-five scripture texts are selected and blended with
the pilgrimage experiences of the author, a retreat master, and well-known writer on prayer.

DISCOVERING
PATHWAYS TO PRAYER   2.95

Msgr. David E. Rosage. Following Jesus was never
meant to be dull, or worse, just duty-filled. Those who
would aspire to a life of prayer and those who have
already begun, will find this book amazingly thorough in
its scripture-punctuated approach.

"A simple but profound book which explains the
many ways and forms of prayer by which the person
hungering for closer union with God may find him" *(Em-
manuel Spillane, O.C.S.O., Abbot, Our Lady of the Holy
Trinity Abbey, Huntsville, Utah).*

DISCE
Seekii   **.50**

Rev. Ch   *ways*
to seek, know and understand God's plan for their lives.
This book is prayerful, refreshing and very practical for
daily application. It is one to be read and used regularly,
not just read" *(Ray Roh, O.S.B.)*.

THE BORN-AGAIN CATHOLIC   3.95

Albert H. Boudreau. This book presents an authoritative
imprimatur treatment of today's most interesting
religious issue. The author, a Catholic layman, looks at
Church tradition past and present and shows that the
born-again experience is not only valid, but actually is
Catholic Christianity at its best. The exciting experience is not only investigated, but the reader is
guided into revitalizing his or her own Christian experience. The informal style, colorful personal experiences, and helpful diagrams make this book en-
joyable and profitable reading.

WISDOM INSTRUCTS HER CHILDREN
The Power of the Spirit and the Word   3.50

John Randall, S.T.D. The author believes that now is
God's time for "wisdom." Through the Holy Spirit,
"power" has become much more accessible in the
Church. Wisdom, however, lags behind and the result is
imbalance and disarray. The Spirit is now seeking to
pour forth a wisdom we never dreamed possible. This
outpouring could lead us into a new age of Jesus
Christ! This is a badly needed, most important book, not
only for the Charismatic Renewal, but for the whole
Church.

GRAINS OF WHEAT   2.95

Kelly B. Kelly. This little book of words received in
prayer is filled with simple yet often profound leadings,
exhortations and encouragement for daily living. Within
the pages are insights to help one function as a Christian, day by day, minute by minute.